Seven Miracles

Miracles
of Prevailing Praise

Proven Steps
FOR GETTING GOD'S ATTENTION

SANDRA THOMPSON WILLIAMS

WESTBOW°
PRESS
A DIVISION OF THOMAS NELSON
& ZONDERVAN

WestBow Press books may be ordered through booksellers or by contacting:

WestBow Press
A Division of Thomas Nelson & Zondervan
1663 Liberty Drive
Bloomington, IN 47403
www.westbowpress.com
1 (866) 928-1240

Because of the dynamic nature of the Internet, any web addresses or links contained in this book may have changed since publication and may no longer be valid. The views expressed in this work are solely those of the author and do not necessarily reflect the views of the publisher, and the publisher hereby disclaims any responsibility for them.

Any people depicted in stock imagery provided by Thinkstock are models, and such images are being used for illustrative purposes only. Certain stock imagery © Thinkstock.

ISBN: 978-1-4908-7702-0 (sc)
ISBN: 978-1-4908-7703-7 (hc)
ISBN: 978-1-4908-7701-3 (e)

Library of Congress Control Number: 2015906004

Print information available on the last page.

WestBow Press rev. date: 05/15/2015

Scripture taken from the King James Version of the Bible.

Scripture quotations taken from the Holy Bible, New Living Translation, Copyright © 1996, 2004. Used by permission of Tyndale House Publishers, Inc., Wheaton, Illinois 60189. All rights reserved.

Scripture taken from the Holy Bible, NEW INTERNATIONAL VERSION®. Copyright © 1973, 1978, 1984, 2011 by Biblica, Inc. All rights reserved worldwide. Used by permission. NEW INTERNATIONAL VERSION® and NIV® are registered trademarks of Biblica, Inc. Use of either trademark for the offering of goods or services requires the prior written consent of Biblica US, Inc.

Now unto the King eternal, immortal, invisible, the only wise God, *be* honour and glory forever and ever. Amen.
(1 Timothy 1:17 KJV)

CONTENTS

Foreword ix

Special Thanks xi

Introduction xiii

Chapter 1: What Is Praise? 1

Chapter 2: What Hinders Praise? 5

Chapter 3: Interpretations of Praise 8

    Favorite Methods of Praise 11

    The First Praise 12

    The Highest Praise 12

The First Miracle of Praise:
Praise Raises You from the Pit

Chapter 4: Joseph's Journey 17

The Second Miracle of Praise:
Praise Rebukes Strongholds from Your Life

Chapter 5: The Jericho Praise 27

Chapter 6: The Bartimaeus Cry 33

Chapter 7: Grief's Horrible Grip 37

The Third Miracle of Praise:
Praise Releases You from Prison

Chapter 8: The Earthquake from Heaven 41

The Fourth Miracle of Praise:
Praise Rejuvenates Your Strength

Chapter 9: Know Joy, Know Strength 51
Chapter 10: The Room of Remembrance 53
Chapter 11: The Secret Weapon of Praise 56

The Fifth Miracle of Praise
Praise Restores Lost Things

Chapter 12: A Silent Voice Restored 61
Chapter 13: Recognizing Who Reigns..................63

The Sixth Miracle of Praise:
Praise Rescues You from Trouble

Chapter 14: Obeying Divine Instructions..............71
Chapter 15: Praise Confuses the Enemy 79

The Seventh Miracle of Praise:
Praise Reforms Lives

Chapter 16: Mary's Radical Praise.....................89
Chapter 17: One Grateful Leper 94
Chapter 18: Suitable Clothes 98
Chapter 19: Daily Exercises of Praise 100
Chapter 20: The Plan of Salvation...................102

About the Author 103

FOREWORD

Honestly, this is a powerful collection of insightful information that Christians should have as a reference. It enlightens us to methods we can avail ourselves for receiving the blessings of God. What a book! This inspirational masterpiece is filled with instructions on how to obtain a miracle. It documents the track record of how God has operated in the past, what he is doing in the present, and what he wants to do in your future. Finally, this book unveils the benefits of prevailing praise, and then quietly invites you to join the party. An absolute must read!

Pastor Frank Thompson
Harvest Church St. Louis

SPECIAL THANKS

I would like to thank Mattie Ewing for her tireless efforts in editing this document. I would also like to thank my husband, family, and church for their support, encouragement, and prayers.

INTRODUCTION

Miracles

Do you need a miracle? Is there a situation in your life that requires supernatural power? Are you facing circumstances that seem impossible to overcome? Then you have come to the right place for help.

A miracle, as defined by *Merriam-Webster's Dictionary*, is an unusual or wonderful event that is believed to be caused by the power of God; a very amazing or unusual event. It is an extraordinary event in the physical world that surpasses known human power. To prevail, according to *Encyclopedia.com*, means to prove more powerful than opposing forces; be victorious. It also means to persuade someone to do something.

Perhaps you are tired, weary, and feel disconnected from God. Are you desperate enough to move beyond your normal resources to get the attention of your heavenly Father? If so, I've got good news. There are untold miracles waiting to be realized through the power of prevailing praise. All that is required is for you to be a believer and willing to offer God praise.

You might be jobless, childless, or penniless. But, dear friend, you are not hopeless. I must be honest. This book is written for Christian believers, those who have put their eternal trust in Christ. However, the family is always open to receiving new brothers and sisters. If you fall into this category, and want to make a change in order to qualify for the supernatural benefits of those who are called by his name, simply flip to the back page of this book where instructions await you. Then come back here, and we will continue. Go ahead ... I will wait for you. The instructions in the back of this book will change your life forever. Selah.

If you have just become my new brother or sister, I would like to welcome you to the family. Hug yourself for me. I love large families. If you were already a member of our super-huge, loving family, I'll hug you later.

I have five siblings. One thing we do in our family is help each other. We bear one another's burdens and cry on one another's shoulders. We also share answers we have received to situations and concerns that we have in common. That's what I am doing in this book: sharing with you what the Lord, through the Holy Spirit, has given me. I have found that sharing is a common activity in the family of our Lord Jesus Christ.

I must confess that I began writing this book ten years before it was published. I thought the information I received that first year would suffice for publication. But I was wrong. My ten-year journey has given me a wealth of understanding through the process that I had to walk, step-by-step, trial-by-trial, and lesson-by-lesson.

We are all called to do something in the body of Christ. I have been chosen by God to sing and write songs that bless him. Many of the Levites in the Old Testament were called to sing unto the Lord. We are called singers, psalmists, praisers, and worshippers.

Within the past year of writing this book, I had an amazing dream. A large, colorful bird resembling a macaw sang a beautiful song to me with many stanzas and ended with three words in an unforgettable vibrato: *God loves praise.* Flabbergasted, I woke up feeling that a heavenly creature had come from the presence of God to give me that great message. Therefore, I feel obligated to say that a bird came all the way from heaven to tell me that God loves praise. I will do all I can to spread that message from heaven to as many people who will receive it.

There are countless benefits from praising God. In this book, I will focus on seven positive performances.

CHAPTER 1

What Is Praise?

Oh that men would praise the LORD for his goodness,
and for his wonderful works to the children of men!
(Psalm 107:8 KJV)

What is praise, and why is there a big deal about it? Here is
an acronym for PRAISE: Powerful Released Acts Involving
Sacrificial Effort.

Naturally speaking, praise has several meanings: to express
warm approval or admiration of; to commend, applaud, eulogize,
and congratulate; and the expression of approval or admiration for
someone or something. *The Merriam-Webster Dictionary* defines
praise in several ways: to say or write good things about; to express
thanks to or love and respect for (God); to glorify. It's a hymn; to
laud, magnify, and resound.

In the spirit realm, however, praise can take you to a different
dimension. I know because I have seen and experienced it. You
may have heard of the fifth dimension. Simply explained,
it is a metaphor for unexplained and unknown aspects of
the universe and of one's self. Perhaps you have heard the
term *sixth sense*. *The Free Dictionary* describes it as a power

of perception seemingly independent of the five senses. As humans, we deal with time, matter, and space. But I want to introduce you to praise. It is not concerned with time or controlled by matter, so it transcends space. It can carry you into a new dimension and introduce you to a new zone. I will speak more on this later.

Praise is more than what we say with our mouths; it is also what we do with our lives. Average individuals relate to life on a natural plane. Although most of us have been taught that we are spirit, mind, and body, we seldom realize that our spirits make up the eternal portion of our triune being. Therefore, our born-again spirits, along with our renewed minds, should lead our temporal bodies. God created us to give him praise.

It is a fact that God loves praise. In Genesis, he praised his own work. He looked at everything he had done and saw that it was good; that it was *very* good. Since humankind was not created until the sixth day, God agreed with himself, within the Godhead and in his own mind, that creation was good, as Genesis reminds us:

> In the beginning God created the heaven and the earth.
>
> And the earth was without form, and void; and darkness was upon the face of the deep. And the Spirit of God moved upon the face of the waters.
>
> And God called the dry land Earth; and the gathering together of the waters called he Seas: and God saw that it was good.
>
> And God saw every thing that he had made, and, behold, it was very good. And the evening and the morning were the sixth day. (Genesis 1:1–2, 10, 31)

We were created in the image of God, and he has given us praise as a weapon, which is used frequently by some but rarely by others. This weapon is very effective. Those who understand how it works have learned to sharpen it. Praise comes in various forms. It can be conservative or liberal, modest or extreme. Extreme praise is known as high praise. Then there is radical praise. We will explore this in a later chapter.

God invented praise. He loves it and rightly so. He is the only one truly deserving of our utmost praise. While the word *hallelujah* is a universal expression of praise, there are unlimited ways to praise God. No Scripture specifies that saying "hallelujah" is the highest praise, but God loves creative adoration. Nothing in the Law mentioned perfumed anointing as praise, yet Mary broke open her alabaster box of precious perfume in order to show her gratitude and praise.

Sporting events are favorite pastimes for millions of Americans and Europeans. We get so excited when our team is winning. It is a proven fact that teams perform better when they hear the fans praising and supporting them. How do we get God's attention? We praise him. He is God and can live anywhere he wants. Yet he is determined to live or dwell in the praises of his people. How awesome is that?

> But thou art holy, O thou that inhabitest the praises of Israel.
>
> —Psalm 22:3

Praise is what you say, feel, and do. These actions can be done independent of one another. Even so, God receives the best praise when we combine them. Consider this. A husband looks at his wife and smiles because he likes what his eyes behold and he feels good that this woman is his wife. End of story. Big deal, you say. Now consider again the above scenario, but this time the husband says to his wife, "I love the way you look." End of story. I bet you like the second story better. Now consider both of the above scenarios. This time, however, the husband gently puts his arms around his wife, kisses her, and says, "I love the way you look." Wouldn't you agree that this is the best scenario?

I may feel praise in my heart all day long, and that's nice. I know it, and God knows it. I can feel praise in my heart and speak it. Now I know it, God knows it, and if others are around, they hear it. Finally, I can feel praise in my heart, declare it, and then do something to prove it. Now I know it, God knows it, and the world believes it! Hallelujah!

Through prayer, meditation, and God's Word, I have found seven miracles that praise will accomplish. Sincere praise accompanies a style of living; our lifestyles should match our praise. Praise works. Praise will change the atmosphere. I invite you to read the following examples of how a changed atmosphere changed lives.

The psalmist proclaims, "Praise waiteth for thee, O God, in Sion: and unto thee shall the vow be performed" (Psalm 65:1). What are you waiting for? Go forth and praise the Lord!

Chapter 2

What Hinders Praise?

It is important to know that praise is a choice. God determined that he did not desire praise from robots. He leaves it up to the people to praise him. However, he gives us innumerable reasons why we should praise him. But if we never praise him, he will continue to receive praise from the angels who cry holy unto him forever.

True praise comes from deep within us, so something is definitely wrong when it does not flow.

I woke up one morning horribly ill. My stomach was causing me great pain, with all the symptoms of what I self-diagnosed as food poisoning. I tried taking a home remedy to soothe the pain and even tried baking soda. When nothing helped, I called my mother. She had retired from nursing but was great at diagnosing health problems. She determined that I needed to get to the emergency room.

Since I was paralyzed by pain, I obeyed without a fight, and she and my brother took me to the emergency room. After the doctor did an initial assessment and gave me something to relieve the pain, he took an X-ray. While waiting for the results, I decided it was probably the flu.

However, when the doctor returned, much to my surprise, he told me I had a bowel obstruction. A what? I hardly had a chance to catch my breath before two nursing attendants came in and forced tubes down my nose. This was the beginning of a two-week nightmare in the hospital. I was scheduled for surgery the next day to have a significant piece of my intestine removed.

Without surgery, not only would I have been unable to eat, but I also would not have lived. In the very center of my body everything had come to a halt. I went ten days without food. I couldn't even receive it intravenously because it had nowhere to go until the blockage was removed and my bodily functions returned to normal.

The point is this: people were made to give God praise, and whenever praise is hindered, there is a blockage. The physician determined that my blockage was caused by scar tissue from a previous surgery, and the foods I had eaten had aggravated the situation. When we don't praise God, there are issues. Obstacles in the center of our beings block our praise. It may be that we are withholding praise because of some previous situations for which we blame God. We think that he is the cause of our grief, debt, or loneliness. So we try to self-medicate our symptoms through entertainment, alcohol, or drugs. However, we only sink further into despair. Only through prayer do we discover that we must give God his due praise. Through praise, doors open and our minds are enlightened. We discover that withholding praise from God can only make matters worse. We must praise him through the good and the bad if we want to continue to enjoy fulfilling lives.

When horrible things happen to us, we always feel tempted to withhold our praise. I can recall one Sunday afternoon driving to a regional church service and honestly feeling that I was making a sacrifice in visiting this church. I had attended my own church that morning and would have loved to spend that afternoon and evening relaxing.

I briefly visited my mother after attending my church. When I left her home I wasn't on the road five minutes before I was pulled over by a policeman. He told me I was speeding and gave me a ticket. Of course, I had a perfectly good reason for speeding those ten seconds or so. I was maneuvering my way from a parking lot in front of some pretty fast-moving traffic because I was trying to avoid getting hit. But I clearly heard the voice of God say, "Don't argue," so I shut my mouth and accepted the ticket. A voice then told me to go home; after all, my day had been ruined. I could have gone home and had a pity party. But another voice said, "Go on to the other church." And that's what I did. I went to church and gave God praise.

About a week later, I was speaking to a young minister and somehow the fact that I had gotten a ticket came up. When I told him where I had received it, much to my surprise, he was the mayor of that municipality and said that he would take care of it! I would not have to appear in court or pay anything at all. There was no doubt in my mind that the Lord rewarded me for offering him praise in spite of the circumstances. If I had withheld my praise, I believe I would never have received favor from the mayor. My reward would have been from whoever attended my pity party.

CHAPTER 3

Interpretations of Praise

It actually takes faith to praise God. Faith helps us believe that praising him is the correct thing to do in spite of our situation. We cannot say we have faith in God unless we give him praise. We cannot say we love God unless we praise him. Faith works by love, and love is an action word. To withhold our praise or let it get away is a huge mistake. The biblical patriarch Israel discovered this in Genesis 37:32–38:1.

> And they sent the coat of many colours, and they brought it to their father; and said, This have we found: know now whether it be thy son's coat or no. And he knew it, and said, It is my son's coat; an evil beast hath devoured him; Joseph is without doubt rent in pieces. And Jacob rent his clothes, and put sackcloth upon his loins, and mourned for his son many days. And all his sons and all his daughters rose up to comfort him; but he refused to be comforted; and he said, For I will go down into the grave unto my son mourning. Thus his father wept for him. And the Midianites sold him into Egypt unto Potiphar, an

officer of Pharaoh's, and captain of the guard. And it came to pass at that time, that Judah went down from his brethren, and turned in to a certain Adullamite, whose name was Hirah.

Jacob was determined not to be comforted. Immediately after that decision, something important happened. The next chapter begins with Judah, who represents praise, leaving. I find this symbolizes what happens when we don't praise God: we lose our praise.

The word *praise* appears at least 248 times in the King James Version of the Bible. The Old Testament Scriptures, according to *Strong's Exhaustive Concordance of the Bible*, were written in Hebrew and the New Testament Scriptures were written in Greek. There are at least nineteen terms in the Old and New Testaments translated as the word *praise* because there are different types of praise. It's like discussing the word *school*. When using the word *school*, we need to know if we are talking about fish traveling in groups or a place of learning. It is also important to know that spellings vary depending on the research.

Strong's lists the following eight terms for praise. There are at least nineteen, but these are more common. I have also included additional definitions from *New American Standard Exhaustive Concordance* and *Worship Basic 101*.

> **tehillah**: praise, song of praise. Original Word: תְּהִלָּה. Part of Speech: Noun Feminine Transliteration: tehillah. Phonetic Spelling: (teh-hil-law'); to sing or to laud; perceived to involve music, especially singing; hymns of the Spirit; example: Psalm 22:3

> **yadah**: to throw, cast. Original Word: יָדָה. Part of Speech: Verb Transliteration: yadah. Phonetic

Spelling: (yaw-daw') Short Definition: thanks; the extended hand; to throw out the hand; to worship with hands extended; example: Genesis 49:8

todah: thanksgiving. Original Word: תּוֹדָה. Part of Speech: Noun Feminine Transliteration: todah. Phonetic Spelling: (to-daw') Short Definition: thanksgiving; extended the hand in adoration, avowal, or acceptance; example: 2 Chronicles 29:31

barak: to kneel, bless Original Word: בָּרַךְ Part of Speech: Verb Transliteration: barak Phonetic Spelling: (baw-rak'); Short Definition: blessed; act of adoration; example: Job 1:21

zamar: Definition melody, song (in praise of Yah) NASB Translation melody (2), song (3), sound ... New American Standard Exhaustive Concordance. song; to pluck the strings of an instrument; joyful expressions; example Psalm 66:2–4

halal or hallel: in formula of worship; compare Late Hebrew הִלּוּל praise, הָלַל id., Hallel – to be clear, to shine to boast to celebrate; to be clamorously foolish; example Psalm 113–118

shabach: commend. Original Word: שָׁבַח. Part of Speech: Verb Transliteration: **shabach**. Phonetic Spelling: (shaw-bakh'); to prostate in homage or worship; example Psalm 95:6

taqa: to thrust, clap, give a blow, blast; Original Word: תָּקַע; Part of Speech: Verb Transliteration: taqa; Phonetic Spelling: (taw-kah'); Short Definition: blow; clap your hands; example: Psalm 47:1

Our God is self-sufficient. He knows that he is great. If man never praises him, God will still be great. According to Ephesians 1:11–12, "In whom also we have obtained an inheritance, being predestinated according to the purpose of him who worketh all things after the counsel of his own will: That we should be to the praise of his glory, who first trusted in Christ."

Praising God is for our benefit. God loves praise and is the only one worthy of constant praise. We must praise God no matter where we are. We were made to praise him.

Favorite Methods of Praise

There are innumerable ways to praise God. He is not hung up on methods, but men have criticized one another for centuries over how to praise God. Some praise him through song, others praise him through dance, and yet others praise him through their imagination. The method of praising God may differ, but the attitude should be the same.

It's hard to find a person in the United States who does not enjoy chicken. I believe nine out of ten non-vegetarians enjoy poultry. Many like it baked, grilled, fried, broiled, stewed, stir-fried, and even barbecued. But however you prepare it, unless it is to the liking of the person for whom it is intended, it will not be well received. In like manner, we must remember that when it comes to praise, it must be to the liking of Jesus. In Isaiah 29:13, God's people were rebuked when God said, "These people come near to me with their mouth and honor me with their lips, but their hearts are far from me" (NIV). From this we can determine that God is more concerned about the sincerity of the praise we offer to him rather than the method.

Praise can produce miracles, but it must be true praise. People are easily impressed with the energy produced by the flesh, but God is not. So sing, dance, play an instrument, run, flip, or shout unto God. But whatever you do, do to the glory and honor of God from a sincere heart.

The First Praise

The first recorded use of the word *praise* in the Bible is found in Genesis 29:35: "And she conceived again, and bare a son: and she said, Now will I praise the LORD: therefore she called his name Judah; and left bearing." However, one of the earliest praises was a blessing from Melchizedek, king of Salem, who said, "And blessed be the most high God, which hath delivered thine enemies into thy hand. And he gave him tithes of all" (Genesis 14:20).

From the very beginning, God's people praised him by elevating him higher than the idol gods. He was lifted to a place of high distinction. If we don't praise him above that which surrounds us, he is not glorified. We must therefore lift him as high as we can.

The Highest Praise

Chapters divide most of the books of the Bible. However, instead of chapters, there are five divisions in the book of Psalms. The word *psalm* is interpreted "praise." Psalm 146 through Psalm 150 have been described by a number of people as "hallelujah psalms" because they each begin and end with "Praise ye the Lord." However, Psalm 104 through Psalm 150 contain the phrase "Praise the Lord," and are often referred to as the Hallel Psalms.

The word *hallelujah* as one word is not technically found in the Old Testament of the King James Version of the Bible. The word is derived from two Hebrew words, *hallal* and *Jah*. "Hallelujah" is thus transliterated as "Praise Jehovah."

To transliterate is to write or print a letter or word using the closest corresponding letters of a different alphabet or language. The word *hallelujah*, however, is found four times in the New Testament, which is written in Greek. But "Praise ye the Lord" or "Hallelujah" occurs twenty-four times in the book of Psalms and is considered by many scholars as the highest praise. This is because no one is higher than Jehovah. It is also considered universal praise because it can be spoken in all languages. No quotable Scripture says this is the highest praise. Rather, it is understood.

I personally think that the angels gave the highest praise when they announced the birth of Jesus, saying, "Glory to God in the highest." You cannot get higher than highest. One compromise is to use the phrases together and get the most out of them: Hallelujah! Glory to God!

The following chapters will give specific biblical examples of the types of praise and the miracles associated with each one.

The First Miracle of Praise:

PRAISE RAISES YOU FROM THE PIT

CHAPTER 4

Joseph's Journey

Within the English word *praise*, five of the letters spell the word *raise*. Praise lifts us up.

When I think of a pit, I imagine a dark, gloomy, isolated, and lonely place. Every person on life's journey will experience pitfalls. Sometimes you fall into a pit, and other times you are thrown into it. Have you been there yet? A pit can represent depression of the worse kind. By that I mean, the pit is so deep that you cannot see daylight. Doesn't that sound horrible? You can be in the pit and hear people discussing why you are in the pit and wondering when you will come out of it. They seem to think you have an invisible ladder.

It is the psychologist's job to determine how you got into the pit. It is your fellow Christians' job to help get you out.

Let's look at the story of an Old Testament pit dweller. Joseph, the son of Jacob, endured many difficult experiences on the journey to his destiny. He was the favorite son and received preferential treatment from his mother and father. If there is favor in your life, please know that you will have to endure hardship. We all know that favor isn't fair. Receiving favor is the most wonderful blessing, and when we see it in the lives of others, we sometimes resent them, as did Joseph's brothers.

Favor attracts jealousy. Joseph was hand-picked by God to save the lives of many people. That was his destiny. However, the journey from his home of comfort to ruler of Egypt was filled with scorn, jealousy, false accusation, and imprisonment, but finally forgiveness. It began with a literal pitfall. His ten brothers threw him into a pit while they tried to determine what to do with him. In their minds, the pit became a place of holding, but for Joseph, it was a horrible experience.

Some years ago there was a commercial about people who had fallen down and couldn't get up and a device that came to their aid. Joseph had a similar experience except it was God who came to his aid.

God granted Joseph unparalleled wisdom to overcome adversity. A bright future was on the horizon for this young boy. He looked forward to the day when his brothers would admire him. The only problem was that his brothers hated him. So they devised a plot that resulted in Joseph being thrown into a pit and subsequently sold into slavery.

It's possible to dislike someone and take no action against them, but the feelings might show up in other ways. This is where Joseph's brothers were divided. Some hated him enough to kill him, others wanted to hurt him, and still others just wanted him out of the way. Murder was logical but immoral. After all, he was their brother. But selling him to the Ishmaelites would be profitable *and* he would be out of their way.

The names of Jacob's other eleven sons spoke of their important destinies. These names were not conjured up but rather came from great thought from their parents. Their names were Reuben, Simeon, Levi, Judah, Dan, Naphtali, Gad, Asher,

Issachar, Zebulun, Joseph, and Benjamin. God had a master plan for each son of Israel.

Reuben was the oldest son. When his brothers wanted to kill Joseph, Reuben wanted no part of it. Reuben is a symbol of maturity, reason, and strength, and his name means, "see a son," as Genesis 29:32 says, "So Leah conceived and bore a son, and she called his name Reuben; for she said, 'The Lord has surely seen my affliction. Now therefore, my husband will love me.'" Although he gave practical reasons why Joseph should be released, Reuben's position as the eldest son was not enough for his brothers to take heed to him. They did not respect his position.

We sometimes try to reason our way out of situations and think our own strength can do great things. However, Reuben's reasoning provided only temporary safety for his brother in an isolated pit. Reuben represents the fact that God sees. However, it is not enough to say that God sees our situation. Reuben could not save Joseph. The Word of God declares that *"The eyes of the LORD are in every place, beholding the evil and the good"* (Proverbs 15:3, emphasis added). In addition to knowing that God sees, we have been instructed to do something: *"The eyes of the LORD are upon the righteous, and his ears are open unto their cry"* (Psalm 34:15, emphasis added).

Sometime's life's problems cause us to retreat to a solitary place for the sake of survival. People sometimes remark, "He seems to be in his own world" or "She's in a shell." Joseph's time alone in the dark pit gave him the opportunity to think. No doubt he cried unto his brothers and pleaded with them. He may have even promised not to tell his father. But none of his pleadings worked.

In the final analysis, it was Joseph's brother Judah who rescued him from death. Judah means "praise." It was Judah's idea to exchange Joseph for something better. In like manner, praise can do something for us that nothing else can. Praise invites us to exchange our attitudes for something better.

Praise can lift us out of life's pit of uncertainty and disappointment. When we are in a pit, we have a choice. We can sing the blues or give God praise. Those who don't know God choose the blues. They drown their sorrows and sometimes take controlled substances to alter their reality.

Praise has power unlike any other. No matter how dark the day or tired the body may be, praise renews and transforms the mind and the spirit. Once you cooperate with praise, you will be lifted from the pit and begin the journey toward your destiny.

However, once out the pit, Joseph experienced years of ups and downs. He was in and out of jail and was feared and scorned as well as revered. But if he had remained in the pit, none of these things would have happened, nor would he have become the second greatest leader in Egypt.

Thank God for praise. Its power catapults us on our journey. If you are stuck in a situation, use your greatest weapon. Let praise get you out. Open your mouth and praise God. There is always something you can praise him for. He's been good to you in spite of the trouble that has attached itself to you.

Now in order to get out of the pit, Joseph had to extend his arms upward and reach. This position is associated with the *yadah* (yaw-daw) praise. "Yadah" means to show reverence or praise with extended hands.

Praise is the secret doorway that leads to many delights. If you want something that only God can give, you must enter through this doorway. God's servant David instructs us to enter into God's gates with thanksgiving. Thanksgiving and praise go together like love and marriage. If your heart can be thankful, it can find praise.

Some people are shy about praising God, but thanksgiving takes care of shyness. When the heart is full of praise, it will overflow. Those of you who are shy need to use your tool of memory to count your blessings. Start with your health. Whatever your physical condition may be, it could always be worse. Thank God for each limb and for the function of each organ. Thank him for your mind. Thank him for each year of your life and from where he has brought you. Thank him for each time he delivered you from evil. Thank him for each day of your life that he protected you. Now thank him for salvation. Thank him for dying on the cross and for taking your place. Thank him for shedding his blood and covering your disobedience and known and secret sins. You get the idea. As you begin to meditate on these things, your heart will enlarge.

You have now entered the courts of the Lord. When you look around and open your mouth, the first thing you say will be praise. Why? Because you are filled with thankfulness. When people are filled with good things, it spills over into their saying something good. When I have prepared a really good meal for my husband, without my prompting, he feels obligated to say, "That was good." So as our hearts are filled with thanksgiving, our mouths will speak the overflow and bless the name of the Lord. If you set your sights on his goodness, it will overshadow the darkness.

"*I cried unto the LORD* with my voice; with my voice unto the LORD did I make my supplication" (Psalm 142:1, emphasis added). Supplication is a noun meaning: the act of communication with a deity (especially as a petition or in adoration or contrition or thanksgiving). So when we pray, it is important to do three things. First, we must give God his due praise and adoration. Tell God how wonderful he is. The birds praise him, the bees praise him, and man should praise him. Second, we must forgive,

21

as Mark 11:25 says, "And when ye stand praying, forgive, if ye have ought against any: that your Father also which is in heaven may forgive you your trespasses." And third, we must include thanksgiving in our prayer to show God that we are grateful for what he has done for us. Thanksgiving puts us in the correct frame of mind. The apostle Paul instructs us in 1 Thessalonians 5:17: "In every thing give thinks: for this is the will of God in Christ Jesus concerning you."

My friend, if you are in that dark place and feel alone, look up. Praise is not far from you. Your deliverance is in your mouth. I remember sitting next to a young lady in a women's conference who appeared depressed and hurt, so I began praying for her and asked her to say, "Thank you, Jesus." As she opened her mouth to say the words, she began to weep. Her praise was bottled up within her, smothered by her circumstances. The enemy of her soul did everything he could to keep her from giving God praise. I don't know why she was in the pit. Life's problems can make us feel like we are drowning. But before the meeting ended, she thanked me for praying for her and said she did receive some relief in attempting to bless God.

David promised himself in Psalm 34:1, "I will bless the Lord at all times: his praise shall continually be in my mouth." I have been in a low place, heavy and disappointed. When we are in a low place, we can't see the sun shining. It's also important to know that if someone does not help us out of the pit, we will be stuck. This is why we need the Holy Spirit, who reminds us to praise God.

When I was a teenager, all my close friends and I had applied at the zoo around the same time for a summer job. My friends were jubilant because they had been hired. But I hadn't received a call. Oh, how I wanted to work there, and I went to God again and again. The last time I got down on my knees concerning the job, the Holy Spirit said to me, "Don't ask me anymore. Thank me for it." You see, praise can take you to a place of faith. The more I praised God for the job, the more I believed it was coming, and every time the telephone rang, I anticipated good news. A short time later, my call came with news that I was hired.

> I waited patiently for the Lord; and he inclined unto me, and heard my cry. He brought me up also out of an horrible pit, out of the miry clay, and set my feet upon a rock, and established my goings. And he hath put a new song in my mouth, even praise unto our God: many shall see it, and fear, and shall trust in the Lord. (Psalm 40:1–3)

If we follow David's instructions above, we will bless God at all times. "At all times" means, even through adversity. This means, when we don't understand what is happening, we must still bless him. This means, when we are in the pit, we must still bless him.

It's interesting that David refers to his pit as horrible. Make no mistake; there's nothing good about a pit. Sometimes creepy crawling things are in there, and you may feel that they are crawling on you. And it is dark in a pit. If you suffer from claustrophobia, you may feel that the walls are closing in, but you cannot escape. If the pit smells bad, you are now dealing with what you see and feel, as all of your senses are telling you that this is the end. As you hear only your own voice echoing in the closed space, you believe you are totally abandoned with no hope of rescue.

Have you ever felt that way? Something horrible happened to you, and you felt alone and saw only darkness. When a pit is deep enough, you don't have any idea if it is day or night. Maybe it's a pit of debt, and you feel that you will never pay off your bills.

Maybe it's a pit of fatigue, and you feel your babies will never stop crying and calling your name or you feel sick and restless. However, David said when he was brought out of the pit, the Lord gave him a new song. And God will for you too. That song will be one of thanksgiving. Others will hear the song born out of your personal experience and will see God, fear him, and trust in him.

What a great purpose the pit serves. It springboards us into evangelism!

The Second Miracle of Praise:

PRAISE REBUKES STRONGHOLDS FROM YOUR LIFE

CHAPTER 5

The Jericho Praise

Did you know there are places God wants to take his people? He has made plans for us and has actually mapped out a road. Jeremiah 29:11 tells us, *"For I know the thoughts that I think toward you, saith the LORD, thoughts of peace, and not of evil, to give you an expected end."* Here, God declares that he knows the plan and is sure of what he wants to do with us. We, on the other hand, are uncertain. Since God does not always reveal to us everything about our lives, we must learn to trust him.

The children of Israel found themselves in a similar situation. They knew they had been chosen by God to be an example to the world and that he wanted to bless them. They also knew he wanted to prove himself through them. But they didn't know what this proof entailed. I have learned through experience that God unveils his plan on a need-to-know basis.

When the Israelites were packing to leave Egypt, they had no idea they would face the Red Sea. If they had known this, undoubtedly some of them would have remained in Egypt. However, miraculously, they got through it and were now facing the last leg of their journey. They had survived the wilderness and were viewing the Promised Land. But there was one problem. They needed to conquer Jericho. The city was considered a stronghold.

A stronghold is a place fortified to protect it against attack; a fortress; a place where a particular cause or belief is strongly defended. A stronghold can be incorrect thinking or beliefs that resist truth. Many strongholds are in the mind.

I can hear their excuses: "What? Now wait a minute, God. Crossing the Red Sea was one thing, and I appreciate your getting us through that. But you want us to do what?" Yes, they had heard God right; he wanted them to destroy Jericho and everyone in it. That was a hard one. I can hear them further: "Okay, God. Can you clue us in on this one? Can't we just sneak around Jericho and settle in the land? We won't bother them, and maybe then they won't bother us."

When the Israelites left Egypt, they abided forty years in the wilderness, during which time an entire generation of murmurers and complainers had died. God wanted a people who would serve him with their whole heart. They were bound for Canaan, the land that flowed with all the blessings they had heard about. Eventually, God's people would settle in a city called Jerusalem and occupy the surrounding territory. But in order to get to their destiny, they had to accomplish one thing: they had to conquer and destroy the inhabitants of Jericho.

Jericho was an interesting city with many beautiful natural resources. It had natural irrigation from underground tributaries, the weather was pleasant year-round, and it was stocked with fruit trees. Jericho is the lowest point on Earth, 258 meters, or 800 feet, below sea level. It's geographic location was symbolic of it's spiritual deprivation. Compare this to New Orleans, which is between two and seven feet below sea level in different parts of the city.

As a direct order from God, Joshua was to destroy Jericho because the city trusted in fertility gods and had built statues to honor them.

> And the city shall be accursed, even it, and all that are therein, to the Lord: only Rahab the harlot shall live, she and all that are with her in the house, because she hid the messengers that we sent. And ye, in any wise keep yourselves from the accursed thing, lest ye make yourselves accursed, when ye take of the accursed thing, and make the camp of Israel a curse, and trouble it. But all the silver, and gold, and vessels of brass and iron, are consecrated unto the Lord: they shall come into the treasury of the Lord. (Joshua 6:17–19)

Isn't it amazing that God recognizes strongholds in our lives and requires that we destroy them? These are not just temptations; these are areas that will *destroy* us. Why couldn't the Israelites just bypass Jericho? There was plenty of land. Couldn't they just share the land with the other inhabitants?

Let's talk about strongholds that hinder God's plan for our lives. Do you have an idol in your life that is off-limits to God? Is there an unholy desire you have not taken to the altar before God? Is there a secret temptation of the flesh that you have not parted with? Perhaps it isn't a big deal to you. After all, you know people with quite visible habits who seem to be disciples of God. Surely, the small habit you have couldn't be that big of a deal.

I felt this same way. I loved God and was a new disciple. Oh sure, I had some rough edges, but someday God would smooth them out. But that someday came much sooner than I thought.

I was addicted to soap operas. I know what you are thinking: *Really? Is that the largest or strongest addiction you can recall?* Friend, it was more than an addiction. It was a stronghold. I was shut up in the world of soap operas and didn't want anyone to know how badly I was addicted to the dramas. Imagine a young woman who says she loves God with all her heart, but when the weekend comes, she is consumed the entire time with thoughts of what will happen during a thirty-minute television segment on Monday. She dreams and daydreams about the episode and even meditates on it. That was me. Soap operas were a stronghold in my life, and I didn't know how to let them go. Oh, that's just entertainment, you might say. Absolutely. They kept me entertained and entwined twenty-four hours a day. Clearly they were an idol. The flesh loves drama, especially when it is juicy and lusty.

One day soon after giving my heart to God, I clearly heard him say, "Give up the soap operas." In Joshua 6:18, the Lord told Joshua, "Keep yourselves from the accursed thing, lest ye make yourselves accursed." Jericho had to be destroyed because it would destroy God's people.

My friend, we cannot compromise with the Enemy. We must obey God! There is no other way to obtain victory. The only way to receive the blessings God has purposed for us is to destroy the things that come between God and us. When God says that something is accursed, he declares it to be evil.

God does not want his people mingling with the accursed, so he commanded Joshua to destroy them, telling him that God had given him the city: "Now Jericho was straitly shut up because of the children of Israel: none went out, and none came in. ²And the LORD said unto Joshua, See, I have given into thine hand Jericho, and the king thereof, and the mighty men of valour" (Joshua 6:1–2).

Joshua's assignment was to take Jericho, and God's instructions were clear. So it is today. Our Jericho is not a city, but it is still a stronghold. A stronghold is any interference that hinders God's plan for your life, and the only way to get rid of it is to follow God's directions. He knows exactly what it will take to destroy it. We want to devise clever plans and military strategies, but God has told us to praise him. The praise must be constant and extreme when you want to rid a stronghold from your life.

You might wonder how praise can destroy a stronghold. That which is natural is natural, but that which is spiritual is spiritual.

> For the *weapons of our warfare* are not carnal, but mighty through God to the pulling down of strong holds. (2 Corinthians 10:4)

> And the LORD said unto Joshua, See, I have given into thine hand Jericho, and the king thereof, and the mighty men of valour. And ye shall compass the city, all ye men of war, and go round about the city once. Thus shalt thou do six days. And seven priests shall bear before the ark seven trumpets of rams' horns: and the seventh day ye shall compass the city seven times, and the priests shall blow with the trumpets. And it shall come to pass, that when they make a long blast with the ram's horn, and when ye hear the sound of the trumpet, all the people shall shout with a great shout; and the wall of the city shall fall down flat, and the people shall ascend up every man straight before him. (Joshua 6:2–5)

Strongholds vary in the lives of individuals. Some are held captive by addictions, such as cigarettes, alcohol, pornography, drugs, gambling, etc. Many strongholds bring feelings of comfort and happiness. Yet the end result is destruction and depression.

Cigarettes are known to cause cancer, and alcoholism is infamous for destroying relationships and homes. However, knowing the downside to an addiction is not always a deterrent. If you are already hooked, the promises you've made to others and yourself don't last.

The answer to every problem we encounter is found in the Word of God. Jericho was surrounded by an obedient, surrendered people whose leaders knew the only way to conquer that stronghold was through God's instructions. For six days, the Israelites marched once around the city. We, too, must face our situations. The Enemy needs to know that we are not running away. The battle is not ours but the Lord's.

The children of Israel sent out a *shabach* (shaw-bakh), which means to be loud in your praise and to put everything you have into it. It is the sound of triumph associated with freedom and is the attitude of wholehearted praise. This is necessary for those who want to be totally freed from their strongholds.

"When the people heard the sound of the rams' horns, they shouted as loud as they could. Suddenly, the walls of Jericho collapsed, and the Israelites charged straight into the town from every side and captured it" (Joshua 6:20 NLT). It wasn't just the noise and the movement that destroyed the walls of Jericho. It was the power *behind* the noise and movement.

There is a power that praise taps into. That power is able to right whatever is wrong.

CHAPTER 6

The Bartimaeus Cry

When my mother was a young bride, she suffered from stomach ailments that weakened her. One day, she told one of her church mothers about her condition. Expecting the mother to offer a gentle prayer, my mother was stunned by a sudden loud outburst from this mother reaching out to God as if to scare away the sickness. However, I now know that she was sending up a shabach to God. She needed God's help and was unashamed to call on him in all his majesty, praising him as loudly as she could. To my mother's surprise, the pain was gone instantly. God does respond to our needs when we praise him with all that's within us.

Blind Bartimaeus witnessed the release of a stronghold from his life. I find it amazing that he had this experience in the same city of Jericho, as told in Mark 10:46–52.

> And they came to Jericho: and as he went out of Jericho
> with his disciples and a great number of people, blind
> Bartimaeus, the son of Timaeus, sat by the highway
> side begging. And when he heard that it was Jesus of
> Nazareth, he began to cry out, and say, Jesus, thou
> son of David, have mercy on me. And many charged

him that he should hold his peace: but he cried the more a great deal, Thou son of David, have mercy on me. And Jesus stood still, and commanded him to be called. And they called the blind man, saying unto him, Be of good comfort, rise; he calleth thee. And he, casting away his garment, rose, and came to Jesus. And Jesus answered and said unto him, What wilt thou that I should do unto thee? The blind man said unto him, Lord, that I might receive my sight. And Jesus said unto him, Go thy way; thy faith hath made thee whole. And immediately he received his sight, and followed Jesus in the way.

When Bartimaeus referred to Jesus as the son of David, he was reaching beyond the genealogy line. Rather, he was referring to Jesus' Messianic title as prophesied in the Old Testament. Bartimaeus was without sight, but he was not without faith. He saw more than those who had perfectly good vision and recognized the chance to receive his sight from the Son of God. When he was asked to keep quiet, he refused. That's how badly he wanted to see.

Jesus recognized that this man had the faith to go against the crowd and cry unto Jesus with the voice of one who recognized his greatness. Bartimaeus knew what he requested and from whom. He lifted Jesus above a rabbi, teacher, or prophet and praised him as the one prophesied to come. Jesus obliged him and gave him his sight.

Blindness was a stronghold in his life; Bartimaeus knew exactly what he wanted and had no doubt that he could get it. Blindness had held him back, and he wanted release from his condition. Is there a condition that is holding you back? Is there a stronghold over your life from which you wish to be freed? Call on Jesus the Savior and Jesus the Deliverer.

If you are a member of the body of Christ, he is your source for this great power. It is a mystery how it works, but we know it *does* work. The walls of Jericho fell, Bartimaeus gained his sight, and the people of God were more than conquerors. Praise will lead you to victory over every situation, even those that seem impossible. I challenge you to praise God and watch him conquer the strongholds in your life.

In Psalm 47:1, we are instructed, "O clap your hands, all ye people; shout unto God with the voice of triumph." There are three elements in this verse. The first is that faith comes from hearing the Word of God. When we shout, it's not because God is hard of hearing. It's because we need to boldly proclaim how great our God is. Second, we are not making noise just to be making noise. We are lifting our voices to the creator of heaven and earth, saying that our God is King of Kings and Lord of Lords. And third, we are shouting with the voice of those who are victorious, praising a God who cannot fail. We are lifting our voices to the one who made us, ordered our steps, and purposed our lives. We are making a loud noise to the one who has chosen us and has great plans for us. We are excited about the success God has ordered for us. The Enemy cannot hold us in his grip when we praise God. So we continue praising him until we are completely freed from every stronghold in our life.

I responded to the voice of God, saying, "Lord, I will give up all the soap operas except for *The Young and the Restless.*" Friend, don't you think that was responsible? After all, I was a young woman. I needed some entertainment in my life. By the way, have you ever argued with a train? The train always wins.

Joshua was sold out to God, meaning he obeyed God without trying to reason with him. A sold-out person will not try to make provision for the flesh. My argument with God was very short-lived. God will not settle for second place in your life. The conviction of the Holy Spirit convinced me to sell out totally to God, and I am so glad that I did. I have never regretted allowing God to destroy that stronghold. But how did it work? It worked through the sacrifice of praise. I sang songs to God that resonated in my spirit. But be warned: don't sing "I Surrender All to God" if you don't mean it, for God is a jealous God.

CHAPTER 7

Grief's Horrible Grip

Now let's talk about grief, a very unpleasant subject. Since we are all human, we are emotional. Some people are more sensitive than others and therefore appear to be more emotional.

The hands of death extend into everyone's lives. Those who love deeply will often grieve deeply.

King David grieved sorely for his son Absalom, who had devised a conspiracy and led a revolt against his father. Yet when David learned of his death, it hurt him and he grieved for a long time. It's natural to grieve when we lose someone we love and care for. But sometimes we grieve for people we don't know, especially when we hear of a tragedy through the news or social media.

A dear friend of mine passed away suddenly from an illness that began in childhood. She was a lovely individual. We shared a close relationship; she was even a bridesmaid in my wedding. The shock of her passing sent me into grief. I continued to function, but everything felt surreal. I had lost relatives and friends before, but never had I felt this way. Grief had a stronghold on me, and I was not sure how long this would last. However, I sang at her funeral under the anointing of God, which brought relief to many of the attendees who were struggling.

My grief continued for weeks. Then our church hosted a revival, during which I sang a song unto the Lord. I gave a *barak* praise to the Lord, and the presence of God came down to me in a way it never had before. My worship was sincere; my song was both prayer and praise. His presence caused me to lose consciousness in a wonderful way, and soon, I was on the floor, giving God praise.

What happened next was incredible. He took my mourning and gave me joy. I don't know how long I worshipped from the floor, but when I got back on my feet, I was laughing with the joy of the Lord, my grief totally gone. Somehow I knew that the joy I felt was what my friend was experiencing now and forever.

I searched for grief by thinking of my dear friend but could not find it. Instead, I discovered a new dimension in God, as described in Isaiah 61:3: "To appoint unto them that mourn in Zion, to give unto them beauty for ashes, the oil of joy for mourning, the garment of praise for the spirit of heaviness; that they might be called trees of righteousness, the planting of the LORD, that he might be glorified." By giving God praise, he had instantly broken a stronghold in my life. I needed and expected help, but I had no idea that my deliverance would occur immediately.

The next day, I did something I had not been able to do before: I drove by the cemetery, still filled with joy and laughter.

I tried explaining to others what had happened to me. I wanted so badly for them to receive deliverance as I had. However, God decided that they would have to go through the valley of time before receiving their deliverance. I was delivered from an aching grief instantly. This was nothing short of a miracle.

Dear friend, praise is so powerful. It can take you far beyond this galaxy. It can take you directly to the glory of our Father, where there is no sadness, grief, or stronghold of any kind. Praise God!

The Third Miracle of Praise:

PRAISE RELEASES
YOU FROM PRISON

CHAPTER 8

The Earthquake from Heaven

The power of praise is an understated phenomenon. Not enough people know about it. Sometimes the Lord allows us to get into awkward and unusual places so others may learn of this power.

We people of God are affected by the same circumstances as our neighbors. We must deal with debt, troubled relationships, sickness, death, and various other adversities. Over time, we learn that complaining doesn't solve any of our problems, yet only a few understand that praise can deliver us from them. Let's look at a biblical example.

The apostle Paul and his assistant, Silas, were jailed for doing the work of the Lord. They specifically had shut down a soothsaying or fortunetelling business by casting a demon from a young woman. Could God have prevented their incarceration? Absolutely. So why did he allow it? Let's review the Scriptures. Acts 16:16–25 says,

> And it came to pass, as we went to prayer, a certain damsel possessed with a spirit of divination met us, which brought her masters much gain by soothsaying: The same followed Paul and us, and cried, saying,

41

These men are the servants of the most high God, which shew unto us the way of salvation. And this did she many days. But Paul, being grieved, turned and said to the spirit, I command thee in the name of Jesus Christ to come out of her. And he came out the same hour. And when her masters saw that the hope of their gains was gone, they caught Paul and Silas, and drew them into the marketplace unto the rulers, And brought them to the magistrates, saying, These men, being Jews, do exceedingly trouble our city, And teach customs, which are not lawful for us to receive, neither to observe, being Romans. And the multitude rose up together against them: and the magistrates rent off their clothes, and commanded to beat them. And when they had laid many stripes upon them, they cast them into prison, charging the jailor to keep them safely: Who, having received such a charge, thrust them into the inner prison, and made their feet fast in the stocks. And at midnight Paul and Silas prayed, and sang praises unto God: and the prisoners heard them.

God can be praised in two ways: an intimate praise when we are alone and a public praise when we are around others. In fact, we are to live lives of praise. When Paul and Silas were in the jail at Philippi, they prayed and sang in spite of those who were among them. Scripture is not clear if the other prisoners were separate from them or if they were in the same cell. But it is clear that the prisoners heard them.

Has your praise ever spilled over to the ears of others? Or are you a silent praiser? Silent praise cannot help those who need to become acquainted with the Deliverer. In fact, in the case of the apostle Paul and Silas, deliverance didn't come until after the other prisoners had heard them praying and singing. It's just possible that the earthquake of your deliverance has already been ordered, but its timing might depend on the release of your praise.

When we examine the story closely, we notice that Paul and Silas were evangelizing and making disciples of those who believed in the Lord Jesus and were taking shelter in the home of a businesswoman named Lydia, who already worshipped God. Yet she opened her heart to learn more about Jesus Christ as taught by Paul and Silas. They then baptized her along with her family and everyone living in her home.

After doing this great work, the Enemy sought to destroy the apostle Paul and Silas. A fortuneteller began following them and announcing who they were. There was nothing wrong with what she said but rather the annoying way she said it. When Paul could stand it no longer, he rebuked the demonic spirit from her, taking away her power to tell fortunes and thus affecting the livelihood of her managers. They angrily grabbed Paul and Silas, took them to the rulers, and accused them of disrupting the city's customs. In a mob scene, Paul and Silas were sentenced to a public beating and then thrown in jail.

I don't know about you, but the average Christian would not be happy about this turn of events. Have you done a good deed or a work for God and it turned out poorly? Perhaps you were trying to feed the poor and you were robbed. Or maybe you took in a homeless individual and he disrespected your home. Maybe you gave a large sum of money to a worthy cause and were accused of only wanting a tax deduction. Or you may have tried to share Christ with coworkers and they accused you of thinking you were better than them. Whatever happened seemed to follow the good deed you had done. In the final analysis, you, like Paul and Silas, were put into a cell. You have been wounded and are now nursing your wounds.

But, my friend, you have a choice. You can become negative and say, "The next time, I'll let someone else reach out to the poor." Or you can choose to stay with a positive attitude. If so, you will automatically praise God for the experience. When you obey God, he will get the glory. You may not see or understand the results immediately, but in the end God will be honored.

Paul and Silas waited until midnight to pray. Perhaps they were not able to freely pray until the guard was asleep. They were in the inner prison and were probably cast into a cell just for them. This inner prison also represents isolation. When your good deed turns out poorly, you, too, can feel very alone and start doubting. How could God allow you to suffer such embarrassing punishment? Did you misunderstand the voice of God? Did you clearly follow his lead? Many voices will question you. The Word of God tell us in 2 Timothy 3:12: "Yea, and all that will live godly in Christ Jesus shall suffer persecution."

But if you know within yourself that you did the work for the glory of God, do what the disciples did: pray and sing praises. For according to Romans 8:28: "And we know that all things work together for good to them that love God, to them who are the called according to his purpose."

Friend, there is no need to beat yourself up when you land in prison. It is always more productive to talk to the Father. Your "get out of jail" card will come through prayer and praise. I don't know if Paul prayed and Silas sang or vice versa. I don't know if they sang a hand-clapping, foot-stomping song or a hymn. I don't know if it had two verses and a chorus or was only one stanza. But this I do know: they sang the song unto God. They lifted their voices unto the King of Kings. I am so glad they didn't sing the blues, where there is no deliverance. Deliverance from prison comes through praise.

When God is praised, the spirit of oppression must leave. God received the prayer and praise of Paul and Silas, and his "amen" manifested through an earthquake! I don't know the kind of prison you are in, but your oppressors cannot hold you if you praise God. Praise him even if it is midnight in your life. When in the darkest part of your journey, lift your voice and give God praise. He will shake the earth to set you free. Your enemies will have to do as the magistrate in Acts 16:35, who told the jailer to "let those men go." And like Paul and Silas, you will not be angry with your oppressors or wish them harm. Instead, you will show the love of Jesus Christ through your witness.

The others prisoners heard the singing of Paul and Silas. Your praise, too, will offer hope to the hopeless. When people see that you can praise God in the inner cell or deep trouble, surely they will begin to praise him too. They will want to see if there is something to this praise thing.

Paul and Silas sent up a shabach, or a loud praise. When I think of them singing, I imagine a hymn, such as "Joyful, Joyful, We Adore Thee," written by Henry Van Dyke to give God glory.

> Joyful, joyful, we adore Thee, God of glory, Lord of love;
> Hearts unfold like flowers before Thee, opening to the sun above.
> Melt the clouds of sin and sadness; drive the dark of doubt away;
> Giver of immortal gladness, fill us with the light of day!
>
> All Thy works with joy surround Thee, earth and heaven reflect Thy rays,
> Stars and angels sing around Thee, center of unbroken praise.

Field and forest, vale and mountain, flowery meadow,
flashing sea,
Singing bird and flowing fountain call us to rejoice
in Thee.

Thou art giving and forgiving, ever blessing, ever
blessed,
Wellspring of the joy of living, ocean depth of happy
rest!
Thou our Father, Christ our Brother, all who live in
love are Thine;
Teach us how to love each other, lift us to the joy
divine.

Mortals, join the happy chorus, which the morning
stars began;
Father love is reigning o'er us, brotherly love binds
man to man.
Ever singing, march we onward, victors in the midst
of strife,
Joyful music leads us Sunward in the triumph song
of life.

Or they could have been singing a hymn similar to "Amazing
Grace."

God simply cannot ignore sincere praise. Some people like to
be flattered, but I don't think it is possible to flatter God. Flattery
is insincere, usually involving compliments that are not true. But
God is good all the time. As David said in Psalm 113: 3, "From
the rising of the sun unto the going down of the same the LORD's
name is to be praised."

We also find in James 1:17: "Every good gift and every perfect gift is from above, and cometh down from the Father of lights, with whom is no variableness, neither shadow of turning." Therefore, God truly deserves our praise and is the only one worthy to receive it constantly.

I am convinced that when we are in prisons or in places that cramp our style or limit our freedom, we need to sing because others need to hear us giving our God praise. God himself will send an earthquake to free us as well as those near us. God desires not only our freedom, but others, for he came to set the captive free: "The Spirit of the Lord God is upon me; because the Lord hath anointed me to preach good tidings unto the meek; he hath sent me to bind up the brokenhearted, to proclaim liberty to the captives, and the opening of the prison to them that are bound" (Isaiah 61:1).

We have been invited to praise our God. Psalm 95:1–3 says, "O come, let us sing unto the Lord: let us make a joyful noise to the rock of our salvation. Let us come before his presence with thanksgiving, and make a joyful noise unto him with psalms. For the Lord is a great God, and a great King above all gods."

We will never know the power available to free us in this life until we give our God the praise that is due him. Acts 16:26–34 tells us,

> And suddenly there was a great earthquake, so that the foundations of the prison were shaken: and immediately all the doors were opened, and every one's bands were loosed. And the keeper of the prison awaking out of his sleep, and seeing the prison doors open, he drew out his sword, and would have killed himself, supposing that the prisoners had been fled. But Paul cried with a loud voice, saying, Do thyself no

harm: for we are all here. Then he called for a light, and sprang in, and came trembling, and fell down before Paul and Silas, And brought them out, and said, Sirs, what must I do to be saved? And they said, Believe on the Lord Jesus Christ, and thou shalt be saved, and thy house. And they spake unto him the word of the Lord, and to all that were in his house. And he took them the same hour of the night, and washed their stripes; and was baptized, he and all his, straightway. And when he had brought them into his house, he set meat before them, and rejoiced, believing in God with all his house.

I love the fact that the deliverance of Paul and Silas came suddenly. When you exercise enough faith to praise God when you are in deep trouble, God is moved on his throne, as his ears are open to the cry of his children. The Enemy would love to give us lockjaw. He knows that if we praise God, he will have to take his hands off us. When we begin to speak well of God's wondrous works, God draws near and the enemy flees.

God could have worked through the system, but he chose to overthrow the whole system to rescue his evangelists and did so in a way that everyone would know it was him. His signature was all over the earthquake. The jailer could not resist and asked to be saved. He wanted to be a part of the team where God himself showed his great power. To prove that he was a believer, the jailer washed the stripes of Paul and Silas and took them to his home and fed them. Hallelujah! When was the last time your enemies fed you? It pays to give God praise for his wonderful works to the children of men.

The Fourth Miracle of Praise:

PRAISE REJUVENATES YOUR STRENGTH

CHAPTER 9

Know Joy, Know Strength

Weakness reveals areas that need to be strengthened. Without strength, we accomplish very little in our lives. We need this strength to be a blessing to others who also need to be strengthened.

When we focus on our limitations, shortcomings, and imperfections, we immediately realize our weaknesses. Some of us feel compelled to write about them. Others sing the blues. But these actions are not any good to anyone. How can my weakness help my brother or sister overcome trials in his or her life? If I see an individual down, distressed, and depressed, I certainly wouldn't go to that individual for comfort and encouragement.

The power of praise, however, is a sure way to receive strength. We must understand that there are spiritual laws and natural laws. Naturally speaking, if I am hurt and miserable, I have nothing to offer anyone when in that state. But spiritually speaking, if I am hurt and miserable, I should tap into the law of praise. The Bible clearly proclaims in Psalm 150:6, "Let everything that has breath, praise the Lord." And King David said in Psalm 34:1, "I will bless the Lord at all times." Now, in the natural, this makes no sense. How can someone who feels miserable bless God? How can someone who is depressed speak well of an invisible God?

It's a spiritual law that you have to purposely step into. When you are in a state of unhappiness, grief, or despair, you have to consciously step into a different room. There is a higher plane, and God has already ordained the way out of this miserable trap of weakness, and that is through his Word that tells us to praise him.

There are many excuses as to why we can't feel better. We will be reminded that life is hard, prodded to think about the terrible circumstances surrounding us, and told every negative thing to continue making us feel weak.

However, if we obey the Word of the Lord, we will praise our way out of weakness into strength. Where is the strength? Where does it lie? The JOY OF THE LORD IS OUR STRENGTH! I said, "The joy (the emotion or source of great happiness) of the Lord (the one who has power and authority; a master; a ruler; a governor; a prince; the Supreme Being; Jehovah; the Savior; Jesus Christ) is our strength."

CHAPTER 10

The Room of Remembrance

So how do we get this joy of the Lord? We begin by thinking about his goodness. Yes, we must step into the room where we look around and see his goodness. Invite yourself to step away from the dungeon of despair and into the room where you see that which brings you happiness. Will you follow me into the room right now? Let's go.

Let's look at the walls. I see pictures of his goodness and snapshots of him and me. There are also pictures of me as a baby. He's holding me. He's even got pictures of me as a young child. He's holding my tiny hand in his large one.

As I continue on, I see pictures of him caring for me when I was sick and him extending his long arms to lift me out of pits. I see angels surrounding me through storms and him hugging me with both arms when I was lonely. Oh, the pictures on the walls of this room are amazing.

Now I see the furniture. There's a chair. It's the mercy seat. I see a table set with what I desire. I open my mouth and give God praise. The joy of the Lord truly is my strength. As I praise him, I feel better. There is strength in this room that I did not know was available when I was in the room of despair. I give God praise again. I praise him with my whole heart. The more I praise him, the stronger and better I feel.

I was physically weak, but the room of remembrance has taken me to a happy place, causing my body to react positively. My muscles have stopped aching, and I begin to feel relaxed. I was bent over, but now I can stand straight. With my feet planted firmly on the ground, I feel strong now. There is something to this joy thing!

I was emotionally wrecked before experiencing the joy in this great room. My focus was blurry. My feelings were ruling me, but now my emotions have come into balance, and I can see things as they really are. Everyone is not against me, and the problems of the world are no longer on my shoulders. I no longer desire to just fade away or disappear.

I no longer feel isolated because I again feel connected to God. I feel his presence and know he is with me. I now understand that I was going through a time of testing. In this room, my purpose is so clear and I understand who I really am: a child of God.

It's amazing what praise can do. Ezra the prophet and Nehemiah, the governor of God's people, understood this. God's people had been disobedient and had fallen away from God's Word. But instead of beating the people over the head with what they had done wrong, Ezra blessed God and read the Law to the people. The people received it and were sorry for their disobedience and rebellion against God. But Nehemiah did not want them to continue to feel sorrowful over their past.

Feeling bad continuously accomplishes nothing. Our God is a God of peace and joy, and his people must serve him with gladness. Look at Psalm 100:2: *Serve* the *LORD with gladness*: come before his presence *with* singing" (emphasis added). A joyful God desires a joyful people. Our joy will become contagious, and others will desire to know our God.

In Nehemiah 8:9–10, we see that he told the people the truth.

> And Nehemiah, which is the Tirshatha, and Ezra the priest and the scribe, and the Levites that taught the people, said unto all the people, This day is holy unto the LORD your God; mourn not, nor weep. For all the people wept, when they heard the words of the law. Then he said unto them, Go your way, eat the fat, and drink the sweet, and send portions unto them for whom nothing is prepared: for this day is holy unto our LORD: neither be ye sorry; for the joy of the LORD is your strength.

Remember, your strength (power and might) is necessary. Therefore, keep your joy. If you have lost it, go to your room of praise. Praise will open up your world to new strength and new possibilities.

Chapter 11

The Secret Weapon of Praise

Growing up in the sixties, I enjoyed war and spy movies. Certainly some were predictable and I could figure out the outcome halfway through. However, in some movies, the secret weapon was kept hidden until it was absolutely necessary to reveal it.

When we read Psalm 57:1–11, we observe a great secret weapon. While David is running from Saul, he comes to a point where he is tired, disgusted, and seemingly at the end of his rope.

> Be merciful unto me, O God, be merciful unto me: for my soul trusteth in thee: yea, in the shadow of thy wings will I make my refuge, until these calamities be overpast. I will cry unto God most high; unto God that performeth all things for me. He shall send from heaven, and save me from the reproach of him that would swallow me up. Selah. God shall send forth his mercy and his truth. My soul is among lions: and I lie even among them that are set on fire, even the sons of men, whose teeth are spears and arrows, and their tongue a sharp sword. Be thou exalted, O God, above the heavens; let thy glory be above all the earth. They

have prepared a net for my steps; my soul is bowed down: they have digged a pit before me, into the midst whereof they are fallen themselves. Selah. My heart is fixed, O God, my heart is fixed: I will sing and give praise. Awake up, my glory; awake, psaltery and harp: I myself will awake early. I will praise thee, O Lord, among the people: I will sing unto thee among the nations. For thy mercy is great unto the heavens, and thy truth unto the clouds. Be thou exalted, O God, above the heavens: let thy glory be above all the earth.

I love where David says, "I will cry unto God that performeth all things for me" and declares that God will "send from heaven" and save him (v. 2). Despite the fact that he is tired, he uses his remaining energy to say that his God will help him, that God would "send forth his mercy and his truth" (v. 3).

It's so good to know that God has taken the foolish things and has confounded the wise. When King David fled from Saul, he had no idea that he would be on the run for years. Many scholars believe he ran and hid for approximately eight years. During that time, David was totally dependent on God for help.

David mentions his enemies in verse four but then he returns to giving God praise. By the time he gets to verse seven, he knows what he must do: send up a *zamar* (zaw-mar) praise. In this praise, an instrument is used to give glory to God. It literally means to pluck the strings and to celebrate in song and music. It appears that while David is exalting God, the Lord drops into his spirit what he must do. The answer is in the praise!

I like to compare Heinz 57 sauce with Psalm 57 because they both contain secrets. One is a secret blend of herbs and spices, and the other is a secret weapon of praise to God by waking up instruments that have been set aside. In verse eight, David tells his instruments, the psaltery and the harp, to wake up. The psaltery is a stringed instrument that predates the violin, and the harp is a tall, stringed instrument shaped like the number seven. After David tells his instruments to wake up, he tells himself to wake up early.

When you are weak and tired, you have no energy to play music. But when you desire to play for the God of your salvation, he will give you the strength. David's zamar praise reached heaven, with which he sent a *tehillah* (tel-hil-law) praise. "Tehillah" means to give a spontaneous praise in song from the heart. In verse nine, David said, "I will praise thee, O Lord, among the people: I will sing unto thee among the nations." He then told God that his mercy was "great unto the heavens" and his "truth unto the clouds."

Listen, David's deliverance showed up when he began to praise God. The praise he sent up to his King actually restored his confidence. As he exalted God, he felt that the Lord his God would protect and help him to escape. Do you think God honored David? Of course he did! Friend, God dwells in the praise! He is listening for what you will speak about him. He is ready and waiting to help you gain the strength you need to overcome whatever trial or battle you are facing.

Perhaps you are not a musician, but can you clap your hands? Hosea 11:12 says, "Judah yet ruleth with God, and is faithful with the saints." Remember, Judah means praise! Praise gets the attention of God when nothing else seems to work. In Psalm 138:3, David declares, "In the day when I cried thou answeredst me, and strengthenedst me with strength in my soul."

58

The Fifth Miracle of Praise

PRAISE RESTORES
LOST THINGS

Chapter 12

A Silent Voice Restored

For I will **restore** health unto thee, and I will heal thee of thy wounds, saith the Lord; because they called thee an Outcast, saying, This is Zion, whom no man seeketh after. (Jeremiah 30:17, emphasis added)

O Lord, thou art my God, I will exalt thee, I will praise thy name; for thou hast done wonderful things; thy counsels of old are faithfulness and truth. (Isaiah 25:1)

He **restore**th my soul: he leadeth me in the paths of righteousness for his name's sake. (Psalm 23:3, emphasis added)

And my tongue shall speak of thy righteousness and of thy praise all the day long. (Psalm 35:28)

Have you ever lost something valuable? I define "valuable" as anything that is important to you. I've lost jewelry, glasses, keys, and many more things than I can recall.

Once I lost something that I couldn't replace: my voice. You're probably thinking that this was not a big deal, and for many it wasn't. But my voice was my weapon of defense. I used it to sing unto the Lord. I had developed laryngitis, and my voice was reduced to a whisper. Then after the laryngitis was gone, I found I had lost my singing voice. I could no longer hit high notes or hold long notes or anything that distinguished my voice from that of others. Devastated, I had to leave the choir.

I was a young college student, and I truly needed my voice. I talked to God about it, truly believing that one day he would restore my voice. Hebrews 11:6 says, "But without faith *it is* impossible to please *him*: for he that cometh to God must believe that he is, and *that* he is a rewarder of them that diligently seek him."

One night, I was singing to the best of my ability along with the congregation in an evening service, "Tell it over again, it's never been told. The half has never yet been told." As I began singing in my mediocre voice, God's attention turned toward me. I know because his anointing came into the song. I began singing in a stronger voice until I was full throttle in the voice I desired.

I was healed in the middle of singing that song. God restored my voice as I offered up a tehillah praise. God accepted my praise and graciously healed me instantly. Hallelujah!

CHAPTER 13

Recognizing Who Reigns

There is a great story in Daniel 4 about a heathen king named Nebuchadnezzer. In a two-sentence synopsis, Nebuchadnezzer literally lost his mind because of pride and arrogance. When he lifted his eyes toward heaven in humility, his reasoning miraculously returned.

Nebuchadnezzer was considered the greatest king of ancient Babylon. He lived between 634–562 BC. He held Daniel and the three Hebrew boys captive in his kingdom and acknowledged that Daniel's God was great. Yet Nebuchadnezzer continued to serve idol gods as his kingdom grew larger and greater. We read in Daniel 4:19–27 that he had a dream that Daniel interpreted for him.

> Then Daniel, whose name was Belteshazzar, was astonied for one hour, and his thoughts troubled him. The king spake, and said, Belteshazzar, let not the dream, or the interpretation thereof, trouble thee. Belteshazzar answered and said, My lord, the dream be to them that hate thee, and the interpretation thereof to thine enemies. The tree that thou sawest, which grew, and was strong, whose height reached unto the heaven,

and the sight thereof to all the earth; Whose leaves were fair, and the fruit thereof much, and in it was meat for all; under which the beasts of the field dwelt, and upon whose branches the fowls of the heaven had their habitation: It is thou, O king, that art grown and become strong: for thy greatness is grown, and reacheth unto heaven, and thy dominion to the end of the earth. And whereas the king saw a watcher and an holy one coming down from heaven, and saying, Hew the tree down, and destroy it; yet leave the stump of the roots thereof in the earth, even with a band of iron and brass, in the tender grass of the field; and let it be wet with the dew of heaven, and let his portion be with the beasts of the field, till seven times pass over him; This is the interpretation, O king, and this is the decree of the most High, which is come upon my lord the king: That they shall drive thee from men, and thy dwelling shall be with the beasts of the field, and they shall make thee to eat grass as oxen, and they shall wet thee with the dew of heaven, and seven times shall pass over thee, till thou know that the most High ruleth in the kingdom of men, and giveth it to whomsoever he will. And whereas they commanded to leave the stump of the tree roots; thy kingdom shall be sure unto thee, after that thou shalt have known that the heavens do rule. Wherefore, O king, let my counsel be acceptable unto thee, and break off thy sins by righteousness, and thine iniquities by shewing mercy to the poor; if it may be a lengthening of thy tranquility.

Daniel explained to the king that the dream meant God would punish the king's arrogance. We know that "God resists the proud but gives grace to the humble." Nebuchadnezzer had seen the power of God in the revelation of the first dream. Yet he continued to live arrogantly because of his great power and influence over other kingdoms.

The Word of the Lord is true. Daniel's interpretation of the king's second dream meant that the king would be cut down like a tree and live like an animal. Still, Nebuchadnezzer continued living as usual for a year before the dream became a reality. One day, while he was admiring all he had built and was glorifying himself, a voice came from heaven saying that his kingdom was departed from him. Immediately, Nebuchadnezzer lost his mind. His ability to reason was taken from him just like someone suffering from mental illness. He was brought down to the level of an animal, even eating grass as they did. His hair grew long like a wild animal's and his nails became like bird claws. All of this happened because he was filled with pride. Eventually, God allowed him enough sense to realize that if he looked to God and acknowledged him as the Most High, he could be restored.

Have you ever lost anything? Perhaps you had something of great value taken away from you. Maybe you were careless in handling your valuable possession or maybe it was stolen from you. You can spend your time lamenting the loss or blaming the thief, but wouldn't it be better to take steps to have your precious possession restored?

Praise can restore things that have been lost. It's true that once time has elapsed, it does not come back. However, truth is higher than facts. God can repay us for lost time. In Joel 2:25, the word of the Lord declares, "I will restore to you the years that the locust has eaten, the cankerworm and the caterpillar, and the palmerworm, my great army which I sent among you."

God promises to make up for lost time. Even when our disobedience caused his wrath, because he is a merciful God, he is willing to restore. When God's people repent of their wrongdoing and give God his deserved praise, he restores that which was lost and makes up for lost time.

Perhaps you are feeling old and believe that your best days are behind you. But if you turn your eyes toward Jesus and begin praising him, you will find that he will restore your will to love life again.

Psalm 103:5 reads, "Who satisfieth thy mouth with good things; so that thy youth is renewed like the eagle's." Who wouldn't want to have the great swiftness of the eagle? Who wouldn't want the ability to see things far off? We bless our God and he enables us to do things those who don't serve him are unable to do. We are not complainers. We see his goodness and our minds recognize that although the outer man perishes, the inner man is renewed day by day. And for this we are grateful.

Not only does God restore time, but God also restores the mind. We live in a time when the world appears to have lost its mind. Creation is praised and worshipped more than the Creator. Man's focus is on himself and the desires of his flesh. However, in Ecclesiastes 1:9, we are told there is nothing new under the sun.

There are many people who need to give God his due praise. If they would only acknowledge God as the Most High and praise his name, they could be restored to a place of honor and good reputation. In Daniel 4:34, Nebuchadnezzar says, "I lifted up mine eyes unto heaven, and my understanding returned unto me, and I blessed the most High, and I praised and honoured him that liveth for ever, whose dominion is an everlasting dominion, and his kingdom is from generation to generation." Then the heathen king delivers a great testimony when he says, "I praise and extol and honor the king of heaven, all whose works are truth, and his ways judgement; and those that walk in pride he is able to abase" (v. 37).

Friend, praise restores the mind. If you are feeling like you are losing your mind due to worry, sickness, or guilt, give God praise. He is no respecter of persons. He did it for Nebuchadnezzar, and he will do it for you.

We have read that praise restores time and the mind. The Word of God also assures us that praise will restore health. Most people who contract the common cold will recover if they rest, drink fluids, and perhaps take cough syrup. But what happens when you have a sickness you can't seem to overcome?

This is what happened to King Hezekiah. The Bible says he was sick unto death. He had a boil somewhere on his body that was killing him. In his own words, he felt he was on his way to the grave and was literally pining away. He turned his attention to God and reminded him that the grave cannot praise him and death cannot celebrate him. He said, "The living, shall praise thee as I do this day." He emphasized the word *living* by repeating it. He wanted to live!

In Isaiah 38:4–6, God, who is forever gracious, sent the prophet Isaiah to Hezekiah with the cure for his illness.

> Then came the word of the LORD to Isaiah, saying, Go, and say to Hezekiah, Thus saith the LORD, the God of David thy father, I have heard thy prayer, I have seen thy tears: behold, I will add unto thy days fifteen years. And I will deliver thee and this city out of the hand of the king of Assyria: and I will defend this city.

Then in Isaiah 38:20, Hezekiah says something remarkable: "The LORD was ready to save me: therefore we will sing my songs to the stringed instruments all the days of our life in the house of the LORD." Hezekiah sent up a zamar praise.

Do you have your own song to sing, my friend? Perhaps it's a song you didn't write but have adopted as your own. It's a great thing to have a song recognized as your own. One of my father's songs was "Don't Forget The Family Prayer, Jesus Loves To Meet You There." My mother's song is "Sweet Jesus, He's The Lily Of The Valley." My song is the hymn, "I Trust In God."

It's time to sing your song!

The Sixth Miracle of Praise:

PRAISE RESCUES YOU FROM TROUBLE

CHAPTER 14

Obeying Divine Instructions

There is an old adage that says, "Never trouble trouble till trouble troubles you," which basically means, don't go looking for trouble. Job said, "Man that is born of a woman is of a few days and full of trouble." (Job 14:1)

Trouble is a seven-letter word that has wings and legs and travels. It takes on many forms and shows up at everyone's door. Sometimes it knocks and we let it in. Yet there are times when we wake up in the morning and it has not only arrived but has also taken up residence. We have automobiles, but trouble seems to often arrive ahead of us. How many times have I heard people say, "I went to work this morning and trouble was waiting for me"? I've also heard, "I went home after work and trouble showed up before I could get out of the car."

Trouble has been personified. Its very name starts with a capital T. It has also become a commodity. I've heard, "I've got a little trouble" or "I'm in big trouble." Trouble never seems to die, but it certainly can leave us and go bother somebody else.

King David was Israel's honored king whose life had plenty of trouble. He didn't have a perfect life or a spotless record, but the people of God still loved him. After being recognized as a man after God's own heart, David knew he would need the Ark of the Covenant for a successful reign in Jerusalem.

Many years before David was king, the Philistines had stolen the ark. With good intentions, David set out on a journey to retrieve it from the home of Abinadab of Gibeah, who lived in the district of Kirjathjearim and whose son, Eleazar, had been sanctified and assigned to keep the ark of the Lord. Excited, David gathered a group of his favorite people and formed a parade of sorts. They put the ark on a new cart and left Abinadab's home, celebrating with instruments.

But there was one problem. We cannot claim to do something in the name of God without receiving God's help. And if we don't ask for God's help, we are doing the work in our own strength and for our own glory. In doing so, God will show us that we indeed do need him. Unfortunately, King David found this out too late.

Abinadab had two other sons, Uzzah and Ahio, who were assigned to escort the ark back to Jerusalem. When they arrived at Nachon's threshing floor, the ox carrying the ark stumbled. A threshing floor symbolizes a place of judgment, but it is actually a place of separation, usually for wheat from straw or husk sometimes called chaff or tares. The edible or good part of the grain is kept while the inedible or bad part is destroyed. Uzzah's life was judged here because of his action. As the ark began to tip over, Uzzah used his hands to keep the ark from falling. However, he was forbidden to touch the ark, which was why the ark had staves for transporting. The Bible says that Uzzah erred and died by the ark because God was angry with him.

The name Uzzah is Hebrew meaning strength. Perhaps he believed he was strong enough to keep the ark from falling to the ground. We may never know. But it is certain that he was not strong enough to defy the commandment of the Lord. Uzzah was not to touch the ark. It was his brother Eleazar who had been sanctified by the town elders to watch over it when it was in their father's home.

King David's journey and expedition had become a disaster. He and all around him were afraid. They were in trouble with God, yet they needed the ark because it represented the presence of God. So they temporarily left the ark at the home of Obed-Edom until they consulted with the Lord.

David was in deep sorrow. His zeal had indirectly cost a man his life. I can imagine how he must have felt. What do you do when your good intentions don't line up with the will of God? David is recorded as asking a serious question: "How shall I bring the ark of God home?" Friend, have you ever felt like that? Have you ever wondered how you can bring the presence of God to your home?

Let's examine what went wrong. We know for certain that God wants to dwell with us, but we need to know his requirements to do so. In 1 Chronicles 13, we find that David had been anointed king of all Israel. Through consulting with God, he was able to win significant battles over his enemies. He was feeling good, and his fame was spreading throughout the land. He then decides to consult with all of his leaders and also with God.

Friend, do you see anything wrong with this picture? During battle, David consulted with God exclusively in regard to fighting or fleeing. But once his fame spread, he decided to consult God *in addition to people.* God instructs people through the counsel of his own will. He doesn't need help. We are told in Proverbs, "In all thy ways acknowledge him and he shall direct thy paths."

But this seemed to be a good idea to David. He was on a winning streak, so how could he lose? First Chronicles 13:2–4 tells us,

> David said unto all the congregation of Israel, "If it
> seem good unto you and that it be of the Lord our

God let us send abroad unto our brethren everywhere, that are left in all the land of Israel, and with them also to the priests and Levites which are in their cities and suburbs that they gather themselves unto us: and let us bring again the ark of our God to us: for we inquired not at it in the days of Samuel and all the congregation said that they would do so: for the thing was right in the eyes of all the people."

But through prayer, David realized his mistake and received an answer to his great challenge of trying to get the ark of God back to Jerusalem. In 1 Chronicles 15:13, David says the breach or punishment came because "we sought *him* not after the due order." Remember, the ark represented the presence of God. David needed to be told the order of procedure so he could properly retrieve the ark without offending the Most High God.

This is what he learned. First, David told the priests and the Levites that they must sanctify themselves, but they should have known better. Any physician knows that he cannot go into surgery without first scrubbing to remove as many germs as he can. The word of the Lord says in Leviticus 20:7, "Sanctify yourselves therefore, and be ye holy: for I am the LORD your God." And Joshua 3:5 says, "And Joshua said unto the people,

Sanctify yourselves: for tomorrow the LORD will do wonders among you."

The company of priests and Levites had gotten so carried away that they had forgotten what was essential, which was what the Lord required. It appears in this case that absence made the heart grow colder.

Second, David was told to appoint singers and musicians. He didn't just appoint anybody. He was selective. The people of God must not believe that music alone is thrilling to God, as he also wants a contrite heart. The attitude must be right, which is why it is important to first sanctify ourselves before him. If we repent of that which we know is wrong, God will reveal those things we are unaware of. We read in 1 Thessalonians 5:22–23: "Abstain from all appearance of evil. And the very God of peace sanctify you wholly; and I pray God your whole spirit and soul and body be preserved blameless unto the coming of our Lord Jesus Christ." Music is much sweeter to God when it comes from a clean spirit. Many people are gifted singers, but if you need a miracle, something more than great talent must be offered to God.

Finally, David was told to make a sacrifice unto the Lord after the musicians were assembled and after the priests and Levites had walked six paces, which was about twenty-seven feet. Six is symbolically the number of man. Man was made on the sixth day, man is to labor six days, and the land was to be sown and harvested for six years. Therefore, the number six symbolizes human weakness, as man can never equal the number seven, which symbolizes perfection. Therefore, man is to go as far as he can go and depend on God for the completion of any act or to perfect it.

The priests and Levites were to offer a sacrifice after six paces. Now we have the winning combination of sanctification, praise, and sacrifice. All praise is to cost something. We are to use energy to praise God, but some people are too lazy to raise their God-given hands, too proud to open their God-given mouths, and too disobedient to repent of any uncleanness in their lives. Yet those who truly need a miracle don't mind clapping their hands, singing out loud, repenting, and joyfully making noise before the Lord, as did the people of God in 1 Chronicles 15:14–21.

> So the priests and the Levites sanctified themselves
> to bring up the ark of the Lord God of Israel. And

75

the children of the Levites bare the ark of God upon their shoulders with the staves thereon, as Moses commanded according to the word of the LORD. And David spake to the chief of the Levites to appoint their brethren to be the singers with instruments of musick, psalteries and harps and cymbals, sounding, by lifting up the voice with joy. So the Levites appointed Heman the son of Joel; and of his brethren, Asaph the son of Berechiah; and of the sons of Merari their brethren, Ethan the son of Kushaiah; And with them their brethren of the second degree, Zechariah, Ben, and Jaaziel, and Shemiramoth, and Jehiel, and Unni, Eliab, and Benaiah, and Maaseiah, and Mattithiah, and Elipheleh, and Mikneiah, and Obededom, and Jeiel, the porters. So the singers, Heman, Asaph, and Ethan, were appointed to sound with cymbals of brass; And Zechariah, and Aziel, and Shemiramoth, and Jehiel, and Unni, and Eliab, and Maaseiah, and Benaiah, with psalteries on Alamoth; And Mattithiah, and Elipheleh and Mikneiah and Obed-edom, and Jeiel and Azaziah, with harps on the Sheminith to excel.

Music changes an atmosphere. Remember, the Word of the Lord says in Ephesians 2:2, "Wherein in time past ye walked according to the course of this world, according to the prince of the power of the air, the spirit that now worketh in the children of disobedience." If you want to change an atmosphere, send out praise and it will blow the Enemy away. When precipitation falls from the clouds, once it hits the atmosphere, it will either rain, snow, or sleet depending on the temperature. If the conditions are just right, it will hail. Precipitation is influenced by wind and temperature before taking its final form.

Therefore, to completely change the atmosphere, the singers were commanded to sing on Alamoth. This is a musical term used in 1 Chronicles 15:20 and Psalm 46 that means to sing by soprano or female voices. They were also told to sing on the Sheminith to excel. It denotes a certain air known as the eighth or a certain key in which the psalm was to be sung. This was the lowest octave.

When we put the Alamoth and the Sheminith together, we have a change in the atmosphere covered by high and low notes. We literally blow the Enemy out of our space when we release these sounds that are dedicated to the glory of God. The Enemy has no room and is paralyzed to do anything because the atmosphere is covered with praises to God!

Notice that during this journey to get the ark, there was no singing about David's exploits. The music was totally dedicated to the Most High God. First Chronicles 15:16 says, "David spake to the chief of the Levites to appoint their brethren to be the singers with instruments of music, psalteries and harps and cymbals, sounding, by lifting up the voice with joy." It's important to know that God delighted in wind and string instruments and even noisy cymbals.

They were not allowed to sing any dry or dead songs; they had to lift their voices with joy. This parade of sorts was filled with zamar praise, which means to pluck the strings and celebrate in song and music. They also included shabach praise because the sounds were loud in tone and the voices were high and low and covered a number of octaves.

Everyone was in order and joyfully went after the presence of the Lord. Oh, what a day that must have been to see the ark of the Lord returning to its rightful people and to its rightful place! The musicians played the instrument assigned to them, and the singers sang and banged the cymbals. Chenaniah was the master of the song who was in charge of this choir and band of sorts. Can you picture this great traveling choir and band under his direction?

The last time we heard of such magnificence of song and music was when Lucifer was in charge in heaven of bringing glory to God. But he failed when he tried to ascend to the throne of God. God had created him perfect, but Lucifer was filled with pride and carried away by his own beauty and talent. Therefore, he was banished from heaven forever.

Chenaniah was giving God a yadah praise, directing and lifting his hands for all to follow. First Chronicles 15:22 says he instructed the song because he was skillful, and much praise went forth. In verse twenty-six, God helped the Levites that held the ark, and then they offered up bullocks and rams. Then in 1 Chronicles 16, David's problem is resolved. His answer was to sanctify the priests, offer praise and worship skillfully, and sacrifice to God continually along the way, which he obediently followed.

Friend, we must do the same. We are to cleanse ourselves from anything we know is wrong and give God our best praise and a sacrificial offering. That offering does not have to be money; it could be time. Whatever it is, it must cost us something to show God that we truly desire him more than anything else. If we don't take the time to do it right the first time, we must take the time to do it over.

CHAPTER 15

Praise Confuses the Enemy

At times, it will appear that you are surrounded by trouble. If God does not rescue you, no one can. This happened to a great and powerful king named Jehoshaphat. Second Chronicles 20:3 says that he prepared his heart to seek the Lord and set up righteous judges and charged them to be faithful and just and to fear the Lord. Jehu, the son of Hanani the seer, chastised him for some mistakes he had made but said there were good things found in him.

One day, the king's enemies, the children of Moab and the children of Ammon, decided to come against Jehoshaphat. When his leaders told him they were close in the land, the king became afraid and set himself to seek the Lord. He also proclaimed a fast throughout all Judah. This scenario reminds me of Psalm 56:3, where King David says, "What time I am afraid, I will trust in thee."

When the people of Judah came together, they asked the Lord for help. Jehoshaphat stood among them in the congregation and said,

O LORD God of our fathers, art not thou God in heaven? and rulest not thou over all the kingdoms of the heathen? and in thine hand is there not power and might, so that none is able to withstand thee? Art not thou our God, who didst drive out the inhabitants of this land before thy people Israel, and gavest it to the seed of Abraham thy friend for ever? And they dwelt therein, and have built thee a sanctuary therein for thy name, saying, If, when evil cometh upon us, as the sword, judgment, or pestilence, or famine, we stand before this house, and in thy presence, (for thy name is in this house,) and cry unto thee in our affliction, then thou wilt hear and help. And now, behold, the children of Ammon and Moab and mount Seir, whom thou wouldest not let Israel invade, when they came out of the land of Egypt, but they turned from them, and destroyed them not; Behold, I say, how they reward us, to come to cast us out of thy possession, which thou hast given us to inherit. O our God, wilt thou not judge them? for we have no might against this great company that cometh against us; neither know we what to do: but our eyes are upon thee. (2 Chronicles 20:6-12)

As we continue reading in verses fourteen and fifteen, we find that the word of the Lord came unto Jahaziel, the son of a Levite, who told them that God said not to be afraid, that the battle was not theirs but the Lord's. Friend, sometimes God will give your answer to the one you least expect. In this case, he did not give the answer to the prophet but to someone in the line of the Levites, who told them that the Lord would be with them. Isn't that all we need to know? We must know that Jehovah Shammah is with us? Jehovah Shammah means "the Lord is there." In Psalm 34:4, David said, "I sought the Lord, and he heard me, and delivered me from all my fears." Once we get rid of fear, we can march into any battle. The Enemy paralyzes us with fear so we don't give God what he expects of us, which is praise.

And Jehoshaphat bowed his head with his face to the ground: and all Judah and the inhabitants of Jerusalem fell before the Lord, worshipping the Lord. And the Levites, of the children of the Kohathites, and of the children of the Korhites, stood up to praise the LORD God of Israel with a loud voice on high. And they rose early in the morning, and went forth into the wilderness of Tekoa: and as they went forth, Jehoshaphat stood and said, Hear me, O Judah, and ye inhabitants of Jerusalem; Believe in the LORD your God, so shall ye be established; believe his prophets, so shall ye prosper. And when he had consulted with the people, he appointed singers unto the LORD, and that should praise the beauty of holiness, as they went out before the army, and to say, Praise the LORD; for his mercy endureth for ever. And when they began to sing and to praise, the LORD set ambushments against the children of Ammon, Moab, and mount Seir, which were come against Judah; and they were smitten. For the children of Ammon and Moab stood up against the inhabitants of mount Seir, utterly to slay and destroy them: and when they had made an end of the inhabitants of Seir, every one helped to destroy another. And when Judah came toward the watch tower in the wilderness, they looked unto the multitude, and, behold, they were dead bodies fallen to the earth, and none escaped. And when Jehoshaphat and his people came to take away the spoil of them, they found among them in abundance both riches with the dead bodies, and precious jewels, which they stripped off for themselves, more than they could carry away: and they were three days in gathering of the spoil, it was so much. And on the fourth day they assembled themselves in the valley of Berachah; for there they blessed the LORD: therefore the name of the same place was called, The valley of Berachah, unto this day. Then they returned, every man of Judah and Jerusalem, and Jehoshaphat in the forefront of them, to go again to Jerusalem with joy; for the LORD had made them to rejoice over their enemies. (2 Chronicles 20:18–27)

It's amazing that God has the answer to every one of our problems. The armies coming against Jehoshaphat and his men looked overwhelming, and it appeared that they would consume them. But God gave Jehoshaphat the victory.

Our answer begins with prayer but always ends in praise. I have heard it said on many occasions that praise will confuse the Enemy. Friend, when you are faced with life-and-death situations, the last thing you are expected to do is praise God. The Enemy scratches his head when you say, "Lord, I thank you in spite of what I am going through."

We must remember that when we are assaulted and attacked by the Enemy, God has planned our escape. In 2 Timothy 1:7 we are reminded that "God has not given us the spirit of fear, but of power and of love and of a sound mind." The Enemy desires to scare us into a negative reaction. But David reminds us of two things in Psalm 56:4: "In God I will praise his word, in God I have put my trust; I will not fear what flesh can do unto me."

Imagine living a life where you constantly praise the Word of the Lord. While you are doing so, you go about your tasks unafraid of the challenges you face. That is the life of a disciplined believer. Our job is to give glory to God.

In 2 Chronicles 20:21, King Jehoshaphat had his singers praise the beauty of holiness, and they marched and sang in front of the army. They said, "Praise the Lord, for his mercy endureth forever." Some people think singing as a worship leader is glamorous. However, when you praise the beauty of holiness, the Enemy gets angry because you are coming against everything that is unlike the Lord, making you a target. It takes courage to sing against the forces of darkness.

Yet something happens when we begin to sing unto the Lord and about the Lord. Even the prayer that King Jehoshaphat offered gave glory to God. He began by asking God some rhetorical questions: if he was in heaven, if he ruled over the kingdoms of heathens, and if he had all-power. This was Jehoshaphat's way of reminding God that he was awesome and that nothing was too hard for him. Listen, when we talk to God about how awesome he is, he agrees with us.

When they began to sing and praise God in verse twenty-two, the Bible says things began to happen. Sometimes if we don't see things happening with our eyes, we feel that nothing is going on. However, something is happening even when we don't see it. Their music and praise was changing the atmosphere. Even though God had never planned their defeat, nothing happened until they began singing and giving God praise.

Years ago, there was a children's television program called *Batman* based on an American comic book. When Batman and his sidekick, Robin, got into a fight with evil men, "Bam!" "Bang!" and "Pop!" appeared on the screen. This is what was happening in the atmosphere. And the same is true of us. When we begin to sing praises to our God, we are combating the forces of evil, disturbing the atmosphere, and causing change to take place for our good.

Singing the blues is a mistake when you need a miracle, as the blues do not give God glory but rather causes a spirit of depression to linger longer. Sing praises to God for his goodness. Sing songs that talk about God's greatness. Sing "How Great Thou Art!" or "How Great Is Our God!" or "Our God Is an Awesome God!" The resulting miracle will blow your mind. Just think. The enemies of Jehoshaphat turned on one another. Friend, not only did God cause the destruction of their enemies through the songs that came up before him, but he also gave the people of God an extra blessing: he allowed them to discover and take the spoils from the camp of the enemy. This included an abundance of riches and precious jewels. It took the king's army three days to gather the spoils.

God delights in recuing his children from trouble. The Psalms are filled with passages that speak of God rescuing his people from trouble.

Deliver me in thy righteousness, and cause me to escape:
incline thine ear unto me, and save me. (Psalm 71:2)

Then they cried to the LORD in their trouble, and he
saved them from their distress. He sent out his word
and healed them; he rescued them from the grave.
(Psalm 107:19-20 NIV)

Bow down thine ear to me; deliver me speedily: be
thou my strong rock, for an house of defense to save
me. (Psalm 31:2)

Whatever your troubling situation, begin giving God praise
for bringing you out of it.

How important is music to God? It's very important. Music is
very powerful; so powerful that it changes the climate in a room.
King David was able to play music and soothe the evil temper of
King Saul. 1 Samuel 16:23 tells us, "And it came to pass, when
the evil spirit from God was upon Saul, that David took a harp,
and played with his hand: so Saul was refreshed, and was well,
and the evil spirit departed from him."

Imagine that a man has dated a woman for some time. They
go out to dinner and have a horrible argument. After a moment
of silence, he pulls out a small wrapped gift and asks the woman
to marry him. How successful do you think he will be? Exactly.
Not successful at all. He obviously doesn't want her to say yes. The
mood is totally wrong. To get the desired response to a situation
we must have the right mood. Music produces a certain mood.
Music affects the person listening as well as the person playing.
Therefore, when we offer music to the Lord, we are changed as
well. The right music with the right words reminds us that we
need our wonderful, awesome Lord.

In 2 Kings 3:9, when Jehoshaphat was on his way to battle, his army and horses and cattle ran out of water. Jehoshaphat sent for a prophet of God named Elisha for advice on what to do, as they were in danger of perishing. When the prophet finally agreed to pray for him, his first order to the king was to send for a musician. "But now bring me a minstrel. And it came to pass, when the minstrel played, that the hand of the LORD came upon him" (2 Kings 3:15).

Why did Elisha need music? Because it is necessary to create the right atmosphere in order to enter the presence of God. David had learned this earlier and instructed others, "Serve the LORD with gladness: come before his presence with singing" (Psalm 100:2). The song must be one of adoration and praise.

Sure enough, God worked a miracle there in the desert for Jehoshaphat, and music and praise played a great part.

The Seventh Miracle of Praise:

PRAISE REFORMS LIVES

CHAPTER 16

Mary's Radical Praise

When we praise someone, we are giving him or her a compliment. Have you praised anyone today? High praise is to exalt someone to a place above us. The highest praise is to tell him or her that he or she is in that exalted place forever. This is why we must always give God the highest praise. He is exalted forever.

Some people never compliment or praise anyone because they believe it decreases their own status. The truth is, their ego won't allow them to praise anyone other than themselves. Can you imagine a world where everyone has something nice to say about his or her neighbor, friend, and even enemy? When you say nice things about your enemy or do something nice for him or her, the Bible says, "Therefore if thine enemy hunger, feed him; if he thirst, give him drink: for in so doing thou shalt heap coals of fire on his head" (Romans 12:20). Your kind act will eventually bring your enemy to shame. God loves kind acts and looks upon them as praise.

Sometimes words fail to express just how much we love the Lord. That was the case of a woman named Mary. She loved Jesus deeply. Have you ever loved someone so much that it was difficult to express your appreciation to them? There are friends who help you out of a jam. There are friends who pay your bail if you are ever arrested or your bills that you cannot pay. There are friends who babysit for you in emergency situations and those who console you in times of sorrow. But have you ever had a friend who actually changed your life? Mary found such a friend who changed her life forever. The people in her town referred to her as a sinner.

Sure, she probably got a good talking-to by those who were concerned about her destructive behavior. She had probably been admonished by family members that she was embarrassing the family name. She may have even tried to change on her own. But, friend, she could not. Then one day, she heard Jesus speaking. I don't know where. She might have been in the crowd when he spoke the beatitudes or maybe among those who received lunch when he multiplied the fish and loaves of bread. Perhaps she was in one of the synagogues when he preached and cast out devils (Mark 1:39). Wherever she saw him, what he had to say was life changing for her. So she followed him and kept up with his whereabouts.

In Luke 7:37, this woman, who up to this point was unidentified, found out that Jesus was going to share a meal at the home of a Pharisee named Simon. It's important to know that Simon represented the leadership of the religious sect and had invited Jesus to be his guest. The other religious people attended as well and all knew the custom of the day: when you have a guest, you wash their dusty feet. This was the least extension of kindness. Friend, if you are like me, when you invite someone to your home, you do your best to make him or her feel welcome. I like to hug my guests and give them a comfortable chair.

But apparently Simon omitted all the niceties of being a host. I'm not even sure the meal was satisfactory. This was an insult to Jesus. If the religious crew did not believe Jesus was the Messiah, perhaps they could have treated him like a prophet. Even an Old

Testament prophet received better treatment. One prophet had been blessed with a room built just for him. Obviously, Jesus Was only invited by Simon so they could interrogate and try to trap him with his words.

But this woman, who was later identified as Mary, had only one agenda. She wanted to show her appreciation for his life-changing words. It's important to note that at this point she was still considered a sinner, but the words of Jesus had touched her heart and reached where no man had before. How do you say thank you to someone like this? Mary decided to sacrifice a special possession. Have you ever sacrificed something of value for a stranger?

Mary wanted to give Jesus the costliest item she owned, a bottle of oil. Nothing was too good for this man whose words had inspired her. Although she was speechless, she was filled with courage. Imagine going into a home, uninvited, as a person with a well-known ungodly reputation. Who knows how well she knew the men in that room? They certainly were well acquainted with her.

But Mary walked right pass them when she saw Jesus. She knew in her heart what to do. She broke open the bottle of oil and poured it on his feet. She saw that his feet were dusty and then wiped them with her hair. A woman's hair was considered her glory, and Mary had used hers to bless Jesus.

But wait ... there's more. Unable to restrain herself, Mary began kissing Jesus' feet. What a display of humility. When was the last time you kissed the feet of a loved one when they were clean, pedicured, and reasonably attractive? To Mary, Jesus' dusty feet were worthy to be kissed and she did so in spite of the cold stares of the other men in the room.

What was Jesus' reaction? Did he push her away or call for security? No, he did not. He received the praise she could not articulate. Her love spoke loudly and clearly. After discerning the thoughts of the self-righteous men in the room, Jesus said,

> And Jesus answering said unto him, Simon, I have somewhat to say unto thee. And he saith, Master, say on. There was a certain creditor which had two debtors: the one owed five hundred pence, and the other fifty. And when they had nothing to pay, he frankly forgave them both. Tell me therefore, which of them will love him most? Simon answered and said, I suppose that he, to whom he forgave most. And he said unto him, Thou hast rightly judged. And he turned to the woman, and said unto Simon, Seest thou this woman? I entered into thine house, thou gavest me no water for my feet: but she hath washed my feet with tears, and wiped them with the hairs of her head. Thou gavest me no kiss: but this woman since the time I came in hath not ceased to kiss my feet. My head with oil thou didst not anoint: but this woman hath anointed my feet with ointment. Wherefore I say unto thee, her sins, which are many, are forgiven; for she loved much: but to whom little is forgiven, the same loveth little. And he said unto her, Thy sins are forgiven. And they that sat at meat with him began to say within themselves, Who is this that forgiveth sins also? And he said to the woman, Thy faith hath saved thee; go in peace. (Luke 7:40–50)

I don't know Mary's full story. I don't know when she became promiscuous. But I do know that after she gave Jesus praise through her most precious possession, her sins were removed and she went away redeemed and reformed. Mary then proved her faithfulness and followed Jesus all the way to the cross. He had given her a new start in life, and she showed her appreciation by following him wherever he went.

When the lips make a statement from an ulterior motive of the flesh, that is flattery. But when the lips make a statement and the heart totally agrees, that is worship. We can say with our lips, "God, you are beautiful," and the statement is true. But do we truly believe it with everything that is within us? Does our heart burn as we say the words? The words may get God's attention, but believing the words will get a reaction from God.

CHAPTER 17

One Grateful Leper

In Luke 17:11–19, ten lepers are in a common colony. We don't know their socioeconomic status, if they were a part of a religious sect, or how they contracted their disease. But this much we do know: they were outcasts, separated from those who led productive lives.

Friend, have you ever felt like an outcast? Think about it for a moment. Have you ever been scorned for reasons beyond your control? Perhaps you have had a child as a result of a rape and no one believed your story. Perhaps you were falsely accused of a crime and were forced to pay retribution. Perhaps you were lied about and stigmatized as a result. Perhaps you have a secret drinking problem, and every time you see someone whispering, you assume it's about you. It doesn't matter what your story is. Life can sometimes group you with others who are down and out.

The Bible says that Jesus was on his way to Jerusalem and passed through Samaria and Galilee. He didn't go anywhere by coincidence. On this day, he entered a village where ten lepers were standing afar off. Can you imagine being a leper in a town where Jesus passed through? They knew who he was. His reputation had preceded him. They called out to him by name. Listen, friend, something happens when you call out to God by name. They got his attention and asked him for mercy. It's important to know that they were not asking for alms or food. They wanted something better. Jesus, filled with compassion, did not refuse them. He told them to go show themselves to the priest. They all went on their way by faith, and as they went, they were healed. I can imagine them pulling off the tattered clothes that hid the distorted portions of their leprous bodies. The leprosy law was clear.

And the LORD spake unto Moses, saying, This shall be the law of the leper in the day of his cleansing: He shall be brought unto the priest: And the priest shall go forth out of the camp; and the priest shall look, and, behold, if the plague of leprosy be healed in the leper; Then shall the priest command to take for him that is to be cleansed two birds alive and clean, and cedar wood, and scarlet, and hyssop: And the priest shall command that one of the birds be killed in an earthen vessel over running water: As for the living bird, he shall take it, and the cedar wood, and the scarlet, and the hyssop, and shall dip them and the living bird in the blood of the bird that was killed over the running water: And he shall sprinkle upon him that is to be cleansed from the leprosy seven times, and shall pronounce him clean, and shall let the living bird loose into the open field. And he that is to be cleansed shall wash his clothes, and shave off all his hair, and wash himself in water, that he may be clean: and after that he shall come into the camp, and shall tarry abroad out of his tent seven days. But it shall be on the seventh day, that he shall shave all his hair off his head and his beard and his eyebrows, even all his hair he shall shave off: and he shall wash his clothes, also he shall wash his flesh in water, and he shall be clean. (Leviticus 14:1–9)

Their excitement must have gotten the best of them. When they saw that they were healed, they could hardly wait for the priest to give them a clean bill of health. However, one of them was not as anxious to be declared clean as he was to mind his manners. He must have been taught that when someone does something nice for you, remember to say thank you. The other lepers may have had good intentions. After all, they were following instructions. Jesus had said, "Go show yourselves," and so they went.

Oh, I imagine it was like the old congregational song that says, "I looked at my hands and my hands looked new, I looked at my feet and they did too." The one leper had a mind to run all the way to the synagogue, but his heart wouldn't let him. You see, he was not only a leper, but he was also a Samaritan. Most, if not all, of the other lepers were Jews. Samaritans were considered half-breeds, and this leper would be reacquainted with a society that scorned his people on a good day. Sure, they both worshipped God, but they disagreed *where* to worship God. Now this Samaritan man had been healed by a Jewish man named Jesus, who was the Messiah. He had much to thank God for and could not continue his journey without offering praise and thanks to the one who had healed him.

We don't know if he tried to convince the others to go back with him. But we do know that he went back alone and that it didn't matter to him. Has God ever done something for you so wonderful that you praised him right on the spot? You couldn't wait to go to church, the temple, or wherever you worship. You did it right there because you were so thankful. That's how this Samaritan felt. He gave God a shabach (loud praise) as he approached him. Then he did what God loves and is looking for: he worshipped God in Spirit and in truth. There was no flattery. He was already healed. He sincerely showed his love, gratitude, and devotion. When he got to Jesus, he gave him a barak praise and kneeled before him. This is the position one assumes when you come before the King. Psalm 95:6 says, "O Come Let us worship and bow down: let us kneel before the Lord our maker."

When he returned, Jesus pointed out that none of the others were found to give glory to God except this stranger. Then Jesus said something to the Samaritan that the others did not hear. He told him, "Rise, go thy way. Thy faith hath made thee whole." All his life, undoubtedly, the Samaritan felt or was made to feel unworthy and like a half-breed, and Jesus pronounced him whole. His life was reformed forever. When Jesus says you are whole, dear friend, your self-esteem should go through the roof. No matter what anyone says about you, the truth is what Jesus says about you.

A whole person is complete and lacking nothing. What a testimony this man now had! He was once a leper, an outcast, and a half-breed. Now he was healed, able to take part in a thriving community, and had everything he needed in order to feel like a real man.

CHAPTER 18

Suitable Clothes

When we begin praising God, we are actually changing our clothes. Have you ever been to an event where everyone was wearing the same color? Perhaps you attended a funeral, and everyone wore black. Perhaps you attended a business meeting, and everyone wore navy blue. What happens when someone walks into either room wearing red? That individual will stand out like a sore thumb.

The same principle is at work when we feel sad or depressed. We are told to put on the garment of praise for the spirit of heaviness. Depression and sadness is a spirit. You can wake up feeling sad and not understand the reason. It doesn't matter if something is wrong or not. We are told to change our clothes. Once we make a conscious effort to give God praise, his Spirit will assist us in praising God. Isaiah 61:3 says, "To appoint unto them that mourn in Zion, to give unto them beauty for ashes, the oil of joy for mourning, the garment of praise for the spirit of heaviness; that they might be called trees of righteousness, the planting of the LORD, that he might be glorified."

Why does the Bible say that praise is comely for the upright in Psalm 33:1? Because it is fitting for the people of God to praise him and perfectly natural for us to sing of his wondrous works. When we don't praise God, we are not being true to who we are as people of God.

There is a portal through the heavens that reaches the throne of God. We reach this place on wings of praise when we send glory to the Lord of heaven and earth. If you want someone's attention, you sing. But if you want someone's *undivided* attention, you must make your song about them. God always inclines an ear to those whose hearts and mouths send up glorious praises unto him, the true and living God.

Praise takes us into another dimension. I remember praising God in my seat during a wonderful service, and when I came to myself, I was dancing in the aisles. However, it felt like someone else was dancing in my shoes. Praise God! Praise takes us out of ourselves and into a glorious state.

Chapter 19

Daily Exercises of Praise

Dear friend, if you need a miracle or just a move from God, try this exercise. From the moment you wake up in the morning until you go to bed at night, find a way to give God praise. Every free thought you have should be dedicated to God. When you are not concentrating on your job, give your thoughts to God. While you are eating your lunch, meditate on his goodness. During travel to and from your job, instead of listening to some idle radio show or mindless music, sing him a song from your heart.

When you go to bed at night, focus your thoughts on his greatness. You will find the more you think of him, the more you will become aware that he is thinking of you. You will begin to see his glory throughout the earth and see him move on your behalf. You will find that you enjoy his fellowship more than your natural food.

You will find it easy to speak of him and to give him praise because you constantly have him on your mind. Begin substituting television shows for reading his Word. You will find yourself falling in love all over again with the God who has saved you from sin and shame. As you live this life of purposeful praise, he will make himself known to you in ways you have never imagined.

Your praise will begin to prevail over all circumstances that ordinarily hold you back in life. Your praise will cause you to triumph during times of disappointing news and you will find you have the victory over all manner of situations. Your joy bucket will be full because you are delighting in the God of your salvation. You will understand the meaning of Psalm 118:6 that says, "The LORD is on my side; I will not fear. What can man do to me?"

With that attitude, you will defy those who think you are going off the deep end. You will find that not only do you love God, but you also love God's people. You love what God loves and hate what God hates. You are always ready to offer up praise. David practiced praising God and determined within himself that he would "bless the Lord at all times." (Psalm 34:1) He invited others to help him when he said, "Let us exalt his name together." (Psalm 34:3) He found fellowship in the body of Christ, where believers have love and praise for God in common.

Here is another exercise. This is especially good for those who have trouble sleeping. Meditate on the alphabet, using each letter to describe God. For example: A—God, you are awesome, B—God, you are beautiful, C—God, you are compassionate, and so on. If you do this, you will enjoy sweet sleep because you are giving God glory instead of focusing on the trials of the day. This also works when you are stuck in traffic. Now go forth and remember to praise the Lord!

CHAPTER 20

The Plan of Salvation

"For God so loved the world, that he gave his only begotten Son, that whosoever believeth in him should not perish, but have everlasting life" (John 3:16). God loves you so much that he made a way through his own Son, Jesus, for you to spend eternity with him.

"For all have sinned, and come short of the glory of God" (Romans 3:23). "And she shall bring forth a son, and thou shalt call his name JESUS: for he shall save his people from their sins" (Matthew 1:21). Friend, you can walk in the newness of life by repeating these words and believing them in your heart. You can truly be born again.

Dear Lord, I confess that I am a sinner and that I need you. I repent of my sins and turn away from them. Please save me from my sins and cause me to walk in your light so I may spend eternity with you and be a witness of your love and grace on this earth. In Jesus' name I pray. Amen.

Lord, I praise you that now I am a part of your family! Hallelujah!

ABOUT THE AUTHOR

Sandra Thompson Williams is a native of Saint Louis, Missouri. She received her bachelor's degree in communication from Saint Louis University and worked more than fifteen years in public relations for educational institutions. She currently works for Saint Louis County Library.

A praise and worship leader at her local church, Sandra enjoys music that reaches the heart of the Father. In 2012, she released her first CD *Songs of Deliverance*. A licensed missionary through her local assembly, she is also a dedicated Sunday School teacher.

Sandra is the author of *Eating the Fruit of Lies* and *The Invocation*, both novels, and *Even Better Than Aunt Harvey's Greens*, a devotional, and coauthor of *Ye Shall Receive Power: The Spiritual Life of Vera Boykin*, a biography. In addition to writing, Sandra enjoys singing, traveling, and discovering hidden truths in the Bible.

Married for twenty-nine years, Sandra and her husband, Leon, reside in Florissant, Missouri. They have three children, Leon, Camille, and Ryan, and two grandchildren, Dominic and Tailor.

Contact Sandra Thompson Williams at SanWill1160@yahoo.com